Well and Smartly Done

Well and Smartly Done

A REMEMBRANCE OF WAR 1943 - 1945

Allen J. Tillery

ISBN-13: 9781981947027
ISBN-10: 1981947027
Library of Congress Control Number: 2017919701
CreateSpace Independent Publishing Platform
North Charleston, South Carolina
Available at amazon.com

"I would set aside a small plot of ground in the center of town as a memorial to war and I would dig ugly holes in the green grass and urinate upon it and defecate upon the ground and fill it with garbage and refuse and let it stink and smell in the hot summer sun and it would remind us of war."

BEACH RED, A NOVEL BY
PETER BOWMAN
1945

Preface

DURING THE SECOND WORLD WAR, a U.S. Marine division consisted of approximately 20,000 troops. When such a division was deployed in battle, these troops were strung out in a line with the rear echelon being that part farthest from the enemy and the <u>point</u> of the most advanced combat patrol being that part of the division nearest the enemy.

The <u>point</u> of a combat patrol is that marine moving in advance of the main body of troops. His function is to make first contact with the enemy - to fire or be fired upon. His function was to prevent a surprise of the main body. So his function was defined by the military texts of 1941.

A marine assigned to the <u>point</u> was assured of a close look at the war. Nothing stood between him and the Empire of Japan but the Japanese Army.

Somewhat in excess of 10,000,000 men and women served in the Armed Forces of the United States during World War II. Of this vast multitude of troops probably less than 300,000 served in, at or near the <u>point</u> of a combat unit. That is, close enough to see an enemy soldier, hear a rifle fired purposefully, feel machine gun bullets rip the foliage over a foxhole or see the dead while they were still warm and the blood yet red. Such was an extremely unique experience. The brotherhood of those who served at the <u>point</u> was few in number.

I do not demean the service or the valor of those who dropped bombs from 30,000 feet, or artillerists and naval gunners, who hurled shells over long ranges, or submariners, who dispatched unsuspecting ships with silent torpedoes or those of our troops who received the bombs, shells and torpedoes delivered by the enemy in like fashion.

There is quite simply a vast difference in the kind of war that one fought. War at the point was personal. As with Cain and Abel, it was man killing man. In many ways, it was yet as it had been at Thermopylae, at Crecy, at Waterloo and at Verdun. Our weapons were more efficient, our transport more expedient – but, the emotion, the loneliness, the fear and sometimes the elation was the same.

To close with the enemy – to force your will upon him – to kill him with your rifle and leave him unburied upon the field. To see him fall - to touch him – to smell him as he rots in the tropical sun. To awake one morning thankful to have survived the night, and to realize that you have done these things, participated in this Armageddon with no feeling of anything but relief to be alive – no remorse – no regrets – no doubts as to right or wrong.

To have violated all of the ancient laws of man so carefully conceived and so artfully promulgated. Thou shall not kill – vengeance is mine saith the Lord.

Vengeance was at the point. Killing was at the point. War was at the point.

For 870 days, from April of 1943 until early October 1945, I served with the U.S. Marine Corps during World War II. This service included tour of duty in the Central Pacific Theater of Operations. While attached to the Third Battalion, 22nd Marine Regiment, I participated in the campaign in the Marshall Islands including the attack and occupation of the Islands of Kwajalien Atoll and Eniwetok Atoll. Later with the Fifth Amphibious Corps, I was assigned to the forces that occupied and pacified Tinian and Guam in the Marianas.

A portion of this time was spent close to the point.

Allen J. Tillery

Arabi, Louisiana
June, 1965

CHAPTER 1

"Niitaka Yama nobore ichi-ni-rei-ya."
(Climb Mount Niitaka, 1208)

Japanese Naval Code message to Combined Fleet confirming
X-Day Pearl Harbor as ooo December 8 (Japan Time)

I have just finished reading an account of the Battle of Gettysburg written some thirty-seven years after those fateful days of early July, 1863. The account was written by a Union Officer, who was an active participant in the battle and who witnessed the terrible action that sent the Army of Northern Virginia down the long road to Appomattox. As a student of the Civil War, I have long recognized the importance to history of such factual accounts written by those who had been involved personally in great events. With the singular exception of those written by Sir Winston Churchill, it is not common for good historical accounts to be written by those who made the history. It has been said that good history cannot be written until at least one hundred years have passed in order to put all happenings in a proper perspective. However, personal accounts of historical events by those who were "eye witnesses" are of some importance to those who in later years write the vast panorama of history.

I discovered while in high school a book belonging to my father, which was entitled Fourteen Hundred and Ninety-One Days in the Confederate

<u>Army</u>, the book had belonged to my Grandfather, Milton Jared Tillery, a Veteran of the Confederate Army. It was written by W.W. Heartsill, a native of Marshall, Texas, and it covered the Civil War experiences of Heartsill while serving with the W.P. Lane Rangers. The book was hand printed by Heartsill in his grocery store in Marshall, Texas. He gave a copy to each of the original one hundred members of the W.P. Lane Rangers. Milton Jared Tillery had received one of the original unbound copies which he later had bound in Shreveport. The book was found among the effects of Milton Jared Tillery at the time of his death in 1909.

This book had some historical significance. I have seen references to the volume in some of my Civil War research. The volume was also of tremendous interest to me because it contained the actual accounts of the actions of my Grandfather while serving the Confederacy. The mere possession of this book and of the knowledge that my Grandfather had served in that lost cause so many years ago, created in me an interest in the Civil War which has continued since my high school days. This interest had led me through many hours of pleasant reading and research and has left me with a firm foundation in American History and a knowledge and understanding of the American past that has brought a deep meaning to my life.

It has occurred to me that I have become so interested in a war that was fought one hundred years ago, that I have entirely overlooked the fact that only twenty years have now passed since I fought as an infantry soldier in the greatest struggle in which man has ever been engaged. We are this year observing the twentieth anniversary of the end of the Second World War. Certainly, it is much too soon to assess its historical significance, but it is not too soon for me to write of my personal experiences as a combatant in that war.

The Second World War was not as romantic as the Civil War. By the middle of the Twentieth Century, war had become too impersonal to be romantic. Mass bombing and long range artillery bombardment could never capture the imagination of Americans as did the sweep of Pickett's charge at Gettysburg or the cavalry charges of Jeb Stuart before Richmond in 1862. From April 23, 1943, until October 5, 1945, I served in the United States Marine Corps in the Second World War. Certainly the experiences of those months will be of interest or significance in later years. As I have enjoyed reading of the experiences of Milton Jared Tillery, an old Confederate Soldier dead these many years, perhaps some day my children or grandchildren will enjoy reading of my experiences as a Marine during the Second World War. It is for them that I am writing this account.

This is not meant to be a precise historical document. It is intended to be an account of my recollections of the Second World War, based upon my experiences as a combatant in that war and extending from my training in the United States to my service overseas in the Central Pacific Area during 1943, 1944 and ending with my discharge at Camp Lejune in North Carolina in October of 1945.

Twenty years have passed since the close of that War. Memory fades and personal recollections are not always accurate and some memories have probably been confused by subsequent reading of accounts of battles and campaigns. A soldier learns quickly that his knowledge of war is limited to that which is within his sight and hearing. It is this knowledge of which I intend to write . . . of things which were within my sight and hearing and of actions in which I was involved in the war.

On December 7, 1941, I was completing my senior year at Fair Park High School in Shreveport, Louisiana. My seventeenth birthday was approaching on January 31, 1942. I do not recall having any particular knowledge at that time of the fact that a war was imminent. History has later revealed to me, of course, that many people in America knew at that time that there was a danger of war with Japan; that our Armed Forces had been placed on an alert in some areas and that the Japanese Ambassador was actually in Washington to deliver an ultimatum to our Secretary of State when the bombs began to fall on Pearl Harbor. The war in Europe was then two years old. As a high school student, interested in world events, I had followed the War in the newspapers and in the magazines with interest. I do not remember believing that the United States was about to become involved in the conflict. I would assume that this was the attitude of the average 16 year old American at the end of 1941.

Extensive army maneuvers had been held in North Louisiana during the summer of 1941. Tanks and columns of soldiers with rifles and machine guns were posted at highway intersections during the war games. These maneuvers were under the command of General Walter Krueger and General Ben Lear. Although these two names would fade into the silent past in a few years, there were several other officers of field grade involved in the maneuvers bearing the names of Eisenhower, Bradley, Patton and Clark, which would become forever identified with the great battles of the approaching conflict. I remember the famous "Yoohoo" incident of these maneuvers involving General Ben Lear. The General had severely reprimanded a group of soldiers who had whistled or "Yoohooed" at some pretty girls passing a convoy. The press of the entire nation jumped to the defense of the enlisted men and this incident was prominent on the front pages of newspapers for many weeks as the press took the General to task for his imposition of this discipline. Needless to say, the discipline was to become tighter in the coming months. The press took great delight at such trivia.

During the summer of 1941, I had worked part-time in a service station in Shreveport for Tad Green. This station was located on Highway 80 at the intersection of the Greenwood Road and Mansfield Road in Shreveport. My father at the time was operating another service station about one block away. Sometime during November or December of 1941, I had again taken a job with Green and was operating the service station on Saturdays and Sundays. I was at this station on Sunday, December 7, 1941. The news broadcasts about noon on that day announced the Japanese attack on Pearl Harbor. War had finally come to America.

Like most Americans, myself and my family stayed close to the radio the following days anxiously awaiting the news reports from around the world. Being only 16 years old at the time, I do not believe that I had any idea that I would be personally involved in the conflict until I was 21 years old. At the time, the draft age for men was 21 years and I had every desire to complete high school and to go on to college before considering service in the Armed Forces.

The War made some changes in our high school curriculum. As an officer in the ROTC at Fair Park High School, I had a greater interest in military training because of the War. In April of 1942, the 204th Coast Artillery National Guard Unit was called into service in Shreveport. Many of the seniors in my high school class were members of this organization and several of them left school to report to Camp Hullen, Texas, with the Coast Artillery Unit. Some of the boys in my high school class contemplated enlisting in the Armed Services immediately after graduation. However, I had planned to go to Louisiana State University upon graduation from high school and I made no plans for immediate enlistment.

Prior to graduation, I had decided to seek an appointment to the Military Academy at West Point. My father was anxious for me to attempt to obtain this appointment. These appointments came through T. Overton Brooks, Congressman from the District representing Shreveport. I wrote to Congressman Brooks on two occasions and also visited with him in his office in Shreveport in an effort to secure his favor for this appointment. I was assisted in this endeavor by Colonel R.W. Holderness, the Commandant of the ROTC forces in Shreveport High Schools. I also received help from General Campbell B. Hodges, who was then President of Louisiana State University. General Hodges was a first cousin of my Grandmother, Mrs. Z.T. Johnston. I was not successful in this endeavor, even though I continued to correspond with Congressman Brooks up until the time I served in the Central Pacific Area with the United States Marine Corps in 1944.

In September of 1942, I enrolled as a freshman at Louisiana State University, planning to study engineering, still with the idea of preparing for an eventual appointment to West Point. I knew that an engineering background would be necessary to pass the examinations required for the Academy. I was not long at LSU when I discovered that engineering was not suitable for me. I had great difficulty with mathematics and also with chemistry even though I had done well in these two courses in high school. I continued with freshman courses in engineering and successfully completed the first semester at the university.

Prior to this time, my older brother, Jim (James H. Tillery, Jr.), had left the University where he was in his senior year in Petroleum Engineering and had enlisted in the United States Marine Corps. He had completed his basic training at San Diego and had gone overseas as a member of the Second Raider Battalion (Carlson's Raiders). We were then beginning to get letters from him from the Pacific describing his activities as a Marine. In August 1942, the Second Raider Battalion had participated in the famous raid upon Makin Atoll in the Central Pacific Area. This was one of the first American attacks against Japanese installations in the Pacific since Pearl Harbor. The Marines were transported to Makin in submarines <u>Nautilus</u> and <u>Argonaut</u>, and made a sneak attack on the Japanese installations on this Atoll. The Marines under the command of Colonel Evans F. Carlson and Major James Roosevelt caught the Japanese completely by surprise and eliminated all of the Japanese installations on Butaritari Island. They retired to their submarines and returned to Pearl Harbor. This raid became famous and was later the basis for a movie. Major Roosevelt returned to the States and presented the Japanese flag captured at Makin to his father at the White House. I remember seeing pictures of this presentation in the newspapers. The Second Raider Battalion was a commando type outfit and we were all proud of the fact that Jim served in such a notable unit. The exploits of the raiders and of their battle cry "Gung-Ho" were to become a part of the legend at the United States Marines.

Late in 1942, Congress lowered the draft age to eighteen years and it became obvious that students like myself would soon face a choice of immediate enlistment in the Armed Forces or of awaiting the draft call. Day by day, students were leaving the university for the Armed Forces. Every time a student left a dormitory room, his room-mates would place a star on the door indicating that someone had left that room to serve in the Army. I began my second semester at LSU in January of 1943, but at this time, my thoughts were not upon pursuing my work at the University, but more upon getting into the War.

The pressure was beginning to mount. Male students in large numbers were leaving the University for service in the War. It was extremely difficult to apply oneself to the research and study required at college when greater things were going on all over the world. The newspapers, the radio and the movies were full of stories of the worldwide conflict. All of us knew that eventually we must serve in some fashion. My father was most anxious for me to remain in college and I knew that it would displease him if I decided to enlist in the Armed Forces without attempting to finish school. The talk in the dormitory was always about the one question of how long we would remain in school and what branch of the service we would go into when the time arrived to go. We were anxious to go. In a few months we would realize our folly.

At this time, I was finding the pursuit of the engineering studies at school extremely difficult. I had begun taking courses in trigonometry and mechanical drawing and I was finding them almost impossible to comprehend. Early in February after much thought and consideration, I decided to leave school for the service. I was apprehensive about telling my father of this decision. I called him by long-distance telephone to tell him of my decision. After listening to my explanation, he accepted it and told me that if that was my decision, then I had his permission to resign from the University and return to Shreveport with the idea of enlisting in the service. I have always been thankful for his understanding. I know that this decision on his part was a very difficult one.

In February, 1943, I resigned from the University, packed my bags and took the train for Shreveport with the intention of enlisting in the United States Marine Corps at the earliest possible moment. When I arrived in Shreveport, I discovered that it was no longer possible to enlist in the Armed Forces. The government had decided that all persons going into the Armed Forces be required to go through local draft boards. In this way, the needs of all of the services could be handled more easily than if individuals were left to enlist in that service which most appealed to them. I went to my local draft board in Shreveport and "volunteered" to be drafted. I was not called by the draft board until early in April, 1943, and consequently I was in Shreveport for about two months prior to receiving the call.

By asking for voluntary induction, I was able to specify the branch of the service to which I intended to be assigned. I had already made up my mind that I preferred service in the United States Marine Corps. I had seen a movie at this time with John Payne and Maureen O'Hara entitled To the Shores of Tripoli. I suspect that this glamorous movie had something to do with my decision to join the Marines. Needless to say, I was soon to find out that service in the Marines was not quite as it was depicted by Hollywood. John Payne had a much easier time than I did and I never did meet Maureen O'Hara in a nurse's uniform.

My notice to report for physical examination arrived in early April, 1943 and on April 22, I reported at the National Guard Armory at Fort Humbug as directed. For the better part of the day, I was directed from one doctor to another, being subjected to the usual questions and probings for the purpose of ascertaining my physical ability to serve in the Armed Forces. About two o'clock in the afternoon, after having spent the day wandering naked all over the Armory, I was informed that I was in good health and acceptable to the United States Marine Corps.

Then came the shocking news that I was to report to the Texas and Pacific Passenger Terminal at 9 o'clock that night for transportation to New Orleans for induction into the United States Marine Corps. I had not anticipated departure so soon. I was soon to learn that the Marine Corps moved swiftly. Along with six other recruits, I said goodbye to my Father and Mother and left for New Orleans as scheduled, arriving there early on the morning of April 23.

After more physicals, I took the oath in the Federal Building off Lafayette Square in New Orleans that afternoon and became Private Allen J. Tillery, USMCR, No. 841175. We were released about 2 P.M. and told to report to the Texas & Pacific Railroad Station on Canal Street at 11 o'clock P.M. for transportation to Boot Camp at San Diego, California. The remainder of that day in New Orleans was perhaps the loneliest that I have ever spent. I had no friends here, no place to go and faced an uncertain future. Seven years later, I would return to New Orleans under much happier conditions.

The train stopped at Shreveport early the next morning en route to San Diego and I said my final farewell to my Mother and Father. Years Later, my

Mother told me that my Father had cried after I left that morning. I had never seen my Father cry. It was not until I had sons of my own that I realized what a difficult task it must have been for my parents to send their eighteen year old son off to the uncertain destiny of war.

———

CHAPTER 2

"You can give your heart to God;
but your ass belongs to me."

A Marine DI
Marine Corps Base
San Diego 1943

Pullmans were not for recruits in those hectic days and we spent three miserable days on a day coach enroute to San Diego and Marine Boot Camp. Arriving in San Diego, we were immediately transported to the Recruit Depot of the Marine Corps Base and delivered into the hands of a Drill Instructor.

There is no human being on the face of the earth who is more powerful, more forceful and more awe inspiring than a Marine DI. I have long since forgotten his name, but I know that for nine weeks, this Marine Sergeant who commanded Platoon 350 of which I was a member was the President, the Secretary of the Navy, the Commanding General, the Pope, the King of England, the Aga Kahn and St. Peter all rolled into one. His word was law, his decisions were final and sixty-five boots lived, moved and breathed by his command. After twenty years, I still recall most vividly the absolute unquestioned obedience accorded to the DI.

It is not necessary to recount all the experiences of Boot Camp. That story has been told many times before and it is all true. Marine Boot Camp is the greatest organization in the world dedicated to the equalization of human beings. The rich and the poor, the educated and the uneducated, the cultured and the uncouth, the handsome and the homely, the strong and the weak, all are beaten on the anvil of tradition, service, discipline and history and unending drill and they emerge as one thing - United States Marines. My service in the Marine Corps was relatively short, but after many years, I still feel tremendous pride at having served in the Corps. Someone once said "The United States Marine Corps is not what it used to be and never was." No greater untruth was ever stated. The Corps is all of that and more.

My platoon was a microcosm of the Corps. By 1943, the draft was reaching deep into the barrel. There were married men in my platoon, some who were at least thirty-five or thirty-six years old. The majority were young – recent high school graduates or men who left college to enlist. They were from all parts of the nation and from every level of society. There were no technical or professional people. These had been sent elsewhere. Most were young and had been poised at the beginning of a meaningful life when the shadow of war crossed their path putting all dreams of careers, marriage and just plain living on hold.

For nine weeks, we labored at becoming marines from 4:45 A.M. to 9 P.M. – from reveille to taps. We were told that we had one objective in life and that was to kill the Japanese. From daylight until dark we expended our energies in this pursuit. There is no such thing as a non-combatant in the Marine Corps and every man is a potential rifleman. Basic training is dedicated to this idea. It takes time to become acquainted with the idea of lectures on how to kick a man in the groin or the best method of gouging out the eye of an adversary. Many new and novel ideas were learned. The best method of dislodging your bayonet from a man's belly is by pulling the trigger of your rifle and blowing him off the end. It is amazing how easy is the transition from algebra and economics to the niceties of killing. Somewhere here is an insight into man's basic character.

Three weeks of Boot Camp was spent on the rifle range at Camp Matthews located in the hills above San Diego. After intensive training with Marine experts, my entire Platoon qualified as Marksmen or better with the M-1 Rifle. We were now qualified to kill at ranges in excess of five hundred yards.

Marksmanship was important to the Corps. A marine was expected to hit any target at which he fired. To fire a rifle accurately was the single most important skill to be learned by a marine recruit. A marine without this skill was a disgrace. We were told this often. Our very lives depended upon the proper use of this weapon. We knew how long it was, its weight, muzzel velocity, name and designation. We cleaned it, nursed it and slept with it. We could take it apart and reassemble it in seconds in absolute darkness. For twenty years after the war, I could remember my rifle number. It was a sacrilege to forget.

After three weeks of training on the rifle range, rifle qualification day was held for each platoon. One could qualify as an Expert (and receive Five Dollars extra pay each month), Sharpshooter or Marksman. Anything less usually provoked a suggestion of suicide on the part of the culprit. I have seen former college fullbacks approach qualification day in a cold sweat. Grown men were known to weep bitter tears when told that they did not measure up.

When I heard that Lee Harvey Oswald was an ex-marine, I was not surprised that he hit his target. He fired at a slowly moving target less than ninety yards away, with a scope that brought it within twenty-two yards. With his training, he could hardly miss. Oswald had qualified as a Sharpshooter at the Marine Corps base at San Diego, fourteen years after my departure.

I qualified as a Marksman. For my purposes this proved sufficient.

Back in San Diego for the final three weeks of Boot Camp, we were introduced to the hand grenade, the bayonet, judo and other assorted tools of destruction.

During June, a B-24 Bomber taking off from Lindberg Field adjacent to our base, suffered a power failure and crashed into a mess hall in which my Platoon was viewing a training film. The plane flew right through the top of the building and crashed in a field nearby. I was struck in the mouth by debris and spent all day at sick-bay. Several men were seriously injured and one subsequently died as a result of injuries sustained in the crash. For many years after that, I had an uncommon fear of low flying planes.

During the second week of June, 1943, my boot camp training ended. We were all given a ten day leave before being ordered to report back to San Diego for advanced training as a prelude to being sent overseas. I traveled by train back to Shreveport spending six days on the train and three days at home. It was a long trip for such a short period at home, but inasmuch as it was the last time that I would be in Shreveport for more than two years, it was well worth the effort.

Upon returning to San Diego, I reported to the Marine Corps Base and was notified that I had been assigned to the Japanese Language School at Camp Elliott Marine Base about twenty miles north of San Diego. I never did discover why I was given such an odd assignment. It did, however, prove to be interesting.

Camp Elliott was an advanced training camp. It served mostly infantry units with a few assorted technical schools of which the language school was the most unusual. There was also a Navajo Indian Language School at the Camp. There were many Navajo Indians in the Marine Corps and they were used in radio communications. The theory was that the Japanese would never be able to understand the Navajo tongue and consequently not be able to intercept field messages.

Camp Elliott was one paved main street about two miles long, being bordered along its entire length by yellow frame two story wooden barracks buildings. I was assigned to one of these barracks. The Japanese Language School consisted of two wooden buildings of the cheapest construction. Each building contained one or two large classrooms and a single office. Each class had a blackboard on one wall and simple wooden tables and benches for the students. It was certainly no better than the little red school houses of one hundred years before. The school was commanded by Major Wolfe and Captain Jewitt, both of whom had lived in Japan and both of whom spoke fluent Japanese. These two officers taught the spoken Japanese. The written language was taught by Lou Yet Ming, a Chinese from the State of Mississippi. There were several other assistants who were noncommissioned officers and who had been previous graduates of the school.

The purpose of this school was to produce interpreters with a sufficient knowledge of Japanese to be able to question prisoners of war in front line positions, so as to give field commanders some intelligence information in combat situations. There was such a scarcity of persons that could speak fluent Japanese that those interpreters and translators with this ability were assigned to division or corps Headquarters. The graduates of the Japanese Language School at Camp Elliott were all enlisted men and they were to be assigned to battalion headquarters so as to handle prisoners in immediate combat areas.

The Japanese Language School was a remarkable educational institution. It had one objective – to teach marines to interrogate Japanese prisoners in front line positions and to read and translate military documents and field orders. The length of the course was three months. In retrospect such a task seems impossible. With the Corps, it was not only possible but successful. We attended classes for seven hours per day, five days each week. We studied independently at the school for two hours each night. At graduation time, I had endured 420 hours of supervised study and 120 hours of homework. All of this time was devoted to one subject – the Japanese language as may be required to converse with prisoners of war. What we learned to say and read was of a military nature. After the war, I discovered that I could discuss the table of organization of a Japanese Infantry Regiment at length, but could not order a meal in a Japanese restaurant. Our vocabulary was highly specialized.

When I first met Japanese soldiers in the Pacific, I had no difficulty conversing with them. With the aid of a dictionary, I could also translate military documents. At one time I knew about five hundred Japanese written characters. With practice my accent and vocabulary improved. By the time I reached Tinian Island in the Marianas in 1944, I was often asked by Japanese prisoners how long I had lived in Japan.

There were about twenty-five marines who began the language school in my class. We studied Japanese from 8 A.M. until 4 P.M. daily and again from 8 P.M. until past midnight. We devoted an hour each day to drill. The Corps would not let us forget that we were still marines. This was during the heat of summer with no fans and no air-conditioning. I do not believe that there were screens on the windows of the classrooms. The work was difficult but extremely interesting. I have a natural aptitude for language and I enjoyed the work. We had a tremendous incentive. If a student failed his tests he was immediately assigned to an infantry company. Every afternoon at 4

P.M. these foot soldiers marched past our classrooms coming in from field exercises, dog tired and covered with layers of red California dust. Our work seemed easy by comparison.

Saturdays were devoted to field problems and the learning of combat tactics. We spent each Saturday fully laden with combat packs and other equipment hiking over the rolling dusty red hills of Southern California, learning the rudiments of fox hole digging, grenade throwing and the other various and sundry tactics necessary to survival in war. We ran obstacle courses, learned to debark from a ship via a cargo net thrown over the side and how to crawl a hundred yards with 30 caliber machine gun bullets being fired overhead. We were now beginning to feel that the war was for real.

We were permitted liberty on weekends and most of us spent these idle hours in San Diego or occasionally if a seventy-two hour pass was available, in Los Angeles. I, together with several friends, discovered LaJolla, which is a small town south of San Diego, located on the Pacific Ocean. LaJolla is a beautiful little town composed of retired individuals living in beautiful homes and magnificent apartments. We had only been there several times when we met at the LaValencia Hotel an elderly lady by the name of Mrs. Hall, who had lived in Japan for a good many years. Mrs. Hall had a particular interest in us inasmuch as we were students of Japanese. We conversed with her in our limited Japanese and spent many happy hours in her home and being entertained by her at the LaValencia Hotel. I have never forgotten the pleasant experiences which this kindly lady contributed to my stay in San Diego.

San Diego was a fleet town and Saturdays and Sundays found the main streets saturated with sailors and marines. It was like Mardi Gras every day. Prices were high, food was scarce and what was there was terrible. I do not have any pleasant memories of San Diego. I am sure that such was not due to the hospitality of the local citizens but to the circumstances of these people being forced to attempt to accommodate and entertain every day thousands upon thousands of sailors, marines and soldiers. No town and no people could really be prepared for such a task. The months that I spent in San Diego were lonely ones for me. I suppose that it takes a while to adjust to the kinds of things in which we were all involved.

Our course at the Japanese Language School was completed on October 15, 1943 and of course there was a great deal of speculation among the troops as to what our assignments would be. We daily came into contact with marines who had returned from the South Pacific and we were daily subjected to the "scuttlebutt" and other tales of what the war was really like. We were anxious to go. It was like a great adventure and now that we were committed we were ready to go where the action was. As I look back now, I wonder how we could have been so anxious to become a part of something so horrible and so useless and senseless.

Shortly before the last day of school, Jerome K. Darden (Fort Arthur, Texas) and I were called into the office of Captain F. O. Wolfe, the School Commandant. Captain Wolfe informed Kirby Darden and me that we had made the highest grades in that graduating class of the language school and as a result, we were to be rewarded by being promoted to Corporal and shipped out. Both of us instantly realized that this was a fine achievement. Promotion in the Marine Corps usually came very slowly and to become a noncommissioned officer within less than one year was almost impossible to believe. We were elated. Captain Wolfe also told us that having done so well in school we were to be immediately assigned to Headquarters of the Fifth Amphibious Corps at Pearl Harbor and that we were to be shipped out immediately. There seemed to be a need for language men in the Pacific and such a need was to move us up front in a hurry.

Shortly thereafter, Darden and I received orders to report to the rear echelon of the Fifth Amphibious Corps which was then located at Camp Linda Vista about five miles from Camp Elliott. Together with half a dozen other marines we were immediately told to pack up and having done so we were shipped up the road to Linda Vista.

Camp Land Vista was the "other side of the tracks". It was a tent camp and was designated as a debarking area to accommodate troops who were awaiting transport overseas. We were assigned to tents which accommodated about four men. The mess hall was a tent with a dirt floor, serviced by a field kitchen with stoves that burned butane gas. There was a row of outside privies located at one end of the camp and at the other end of the camp was a tent containing five showers which were serviced by a boiler that burned wood. Most of us believed that Camp Linda Vista must have been left over from the Civil War. It was about as uncomfortable as a place could be. I do not believe that in all of my combat experience that I ever encountered a camp that had as few luxuries as did Camp Linda Vista. By this time the weather in Southern California was cold. Each tent had a kerosene stove which emitted horrible fumes. I was to stay at Linda Vista for two months preparing for transport to Pearl Harbor. For the most part we did nothing here but prepare our equipment, bellyache and wait for further orders.

On January 2, 1944, we boarded trucks for the San Diego docks. Arriving on the docks, we were marched onto the <u>USS Manila Bay</u> which was a small aircraft carrier called a C.V.E. The <u>Manila Bay</u> was an aircraft carrier built onto the body of a merchant ship. We needed aircraft carriers in a hurry and it was not possible to await the building of the usual heavily fortified Navy ship. The carrier, of course, was not equipped to handle a great number of troops. We were assigned cots on the hanger deck of the ship and all of us slept beneath the wings of the planes on the deck. Late in the afternoon the <u>Manila Bay</u> steamed out of San Diego Harbor and headed south. We joined a convoy and late that afternoon all of the marines sat on the flight deck watching the California coastline and home disappear over the horizon. It would be eighteen months before I would see that sight again.

CHAPTER 3

Operation Catchpole
Eniwetok

———

"Well and Smartly Done. Carry On."

FLEET ADMIRAL ERNEST KING, C.N.O. TO
MARSHALL ISLANDS TASK FORCE
MARCH, 1944.

THE TRIP TO HAWAII WAS pleasant. The weather was good, the sea calm and the Navy food aboard the carrier was excellent. We lounged on the flight deck enjoying the warm sun and began the endless task of cleaning rifles, sharpening knives and in general preparing our equipment for whatever there was out there over the horizon. It took us six days from San Diego to Oahu. There was tremendous excitement aboard the ship as we pulled into Pearl Harbor. It was here that it had all begun for us. We could still see the damaged hulks of the American battleships which had been sunk and damaged on December 7, 1941. This was the first contact for most of us with the actual war. We passed Ford Island and Hickam Field and all of these spots were pointed out to us by the sailors on the ship. We passed the Oklahoma and the Arizona still lying as they were left by the Japanese bombers almost two years before.

The sudden realization that there were entombed in these sunken and battered hulks several hundred sailors and marines who had been killed in the Japanese attack gave many of us pause for thought. Upon arrival at Pearl Harbor, we were immediately assigned to a Transient Center to await further transfer to the Fifth Amphibious Corps which was then being formed under the command of Admiral Richmond Kelly Turner. The Transient Center was a huge complex of tents situated on a hillside amid the pineapple fields. It housed thousands of marines all in the process of awaiting orders to go somewhere. The troops had no permanent duties beyond general guard duty and the necessary task of keeping the camp clean and in proper police. Ennui was the order of the day and it rested heavily upon all of us. Efforts to dispel it were fruitless. Nothing was permanent except the terrible uncertainty of the future. There was at all times an urgency to move west out into the Pacific to the islands beyond the horizon.

The camp was full of marines who were just returning from the campaign in the Gilbert Islands. These men of the Second Marine Division had a few months before made the terrible landings at Tarawa. This was the bloodiest amphibious operation in the history of modern warfare. Almost 1,000 marines died on the beaches of Betio before the atoll was secured. Most of us spent long hours listening to tales of this campaign from the Second Division veterans. These stories sanguine as they were only seemed to whet our desire for a closer look at the war. In a few short months many of us would wonder how we could have been so foolish.

On January 13, 1944 a messenger came to my tent and informed me that a jeep was waiting to transport me to Fifth Amphibious Corps Headquarters at Pearl Harbor for assignment. I did not know why I had been given special attention. When I arrived at the Marine Headquarters at the Naval Base at Pearl Harbor I was immediately sent to the office of Warrant Officer S.A. Guy. It is strange that I still remember this Warrant Officer's name. He was to play an important part in my life when we were to meet again in a few months.

I walked into his office and saw him look up from the typewriter and in a tired voice, say "Son, are you ready to fight this war?"

Having answered in the affirmative, I was told by Mr. Guy that the 22nd Marine Regiment was then aboard transports lying at anchor in Pearl Harbor and that one of their battalions was in need of a Japanese interpreter and hence the reason for my assignment. I was told that orders would be cut immediately assigning me to the Headquarters Company, Third Battalion, 22nd Marine Regiment, and that I was to report immediately with all of my gear aboard a certain ship which would be designated to me verbally and which was then anchored at the Naval Base. As I walked out of the office Mr. Guy asked me if I had been assigned any live ammunition. When I told him I had not, he arranged for me to be issued a number of clips containing live M-l ammunition. Training had now ceased.

After receiving written orders designating my new assignment I was transported back to the Transient Center and given about forty-five minutes to pack my gear. I packed my sea bag, grabbed my rifle and climbed aboard the jeep which was to take me to the 22nd Marines. As we left the Transient Center the jeep driver who knew my situation asked me if I would not like to drive through Honolulu. He remarked rather humorously that this might be the last time that I would have a chance to see Hawaii. We drove rather leisurely through Honolulu and then out onto the road leading to the Naval Base.

I had been told verbally that I was to report to the Commanding Officer of Headquarters Company, Third Battalion, 22nd Marine Regiment, which was then aboard the U.S.S. President Coolidge, at a certain designated dock at the Naval Base. Later that afternoon I boarded the President Coolidge and reported as ordered to the Commanding Officer of the Headquarters Company of the Third Battalion. I was immediately handed over to Gunnery Sergeant Nagazine who forthwith informed all within hearing of his booming voice how useless I would be to his battalion since they fully intended to kill every god-damned Gook that got in their way. He had nothing to say to the enemy.

The 22nd Regiment had been stationed in Samoa for twenty-one months prior to having been assigned to the coming operation. Most of their personnel had shipped out of the states together and had remained with the 22nd Regiment in Samoa since that time. They were for the most part "island happy." As a defense regiment on Samoa they had done nothing but sit, gripe and endure endless training exercises for a long time. Most of them were ready for whatever it took two years to get ready for. They were a clan. Most of these marines had been in the Corps for well over three years, with two of these years having been spent in the South Pacific. A great majority of them were still privates. I was only four months out of boot camp with the rank of Corporal. They did not take kindly to me.

I was attached to the 22nd Regiment for almost four months and I do not believe that I established a close friendship with anyone during that time. These several months were the most desolate time that I spent in the Corps. Had we not been so busily engaged in an actual operation against the Japanese, I am sure that I would have been completely miserable for the entire period of attachment to this very fine regiment. The 22nd Marines was an excellent outfit by Marine standards. They had trained for a long time and they were now committed to an operation which was to test that training in the crucible of amphibious warfare. These men were tough. They had been away from home for a long time. They well knew that the only way for them to return home was to attain victory in the islands to the west.

I was assigned to the B-2 (Intelligence) Section of the Headquarters and Service Company of the 3rd Battalion and given a bunk about three decks below the waterline. During the night the ship departed from Pearl Harbor and when 1 awoke the next morning we were at sea. We were to make an amphibious landing on the coast of Maui (one of the Hawaiian Islands) that afternoon as a part of the final training exercises of the task force. Everyone had been through this type of thing many times and none of them seemed to realize that it was all new to me. I was given no instructions and had to just follow the leader. We made a simulated assault on Maui as directed. It was the first time that I had ever gone over the side of a ship and down a cargo net into a bouncing Higgins boat. It was quite an experience and one that I was to repeat many times in the coming months. We hit the beach, moved inland and were told to dig in for the night. I dug a fox hole, climbed in and did not move until the next morning. The area in which we were dug in was adjacent to an army camp and my fox hole was only about one hundred feet from an army open air theatre where the local troops were watching Bob Hope and

Madeline Carroll in <u>My Favorite Blonde</u>. I went to sleep in my hole that night listening to Bob Hope making love to Madeline Carroll.

We boarded ship again the next morning and sailed back to Pearl Harbor. At Pearl Harbor we were transferred to the <u>U.S.S. Leonard Wood</u>, a United States Coast Guard Troop ship. On January 23, 1944, the Leonard Wood departed from Pearl Harbor and joined a convoy headed west. Every day, more and more ships became attached to the convoy until the entire ocean seemed to be covered with ships as far as the eye could see. Our favorite sport was speculation as to what our objective would be. No one seemed to know where we were going but we all knew that whoever was at the other end of the line was in for a great deal of trouble. As the convoy headed west we began to see aircraft carriers, battleships and cruisers sailing across the horizon. Planes daily made patrols over the convoy and apparently these were from American aircraft carriers doing anti-submarine patrol work.

On February 1st, after nine days at sea, our convoy arrived off Kwajalein Atoll in the Marshall Islands. This was to be our first objective. As we moved into the atoll between two low-lying islands, the battleships and cruisers lying off in the distance began to bombard the islands. For hours we could hear the shells pass over our ship on their deadly journey to the smoke covered islands further up the chain of the atoll. The shelling lasted all day and into the night. Throughout the day, we watched as planes from the carriers flew over the islands strafing and dropping bombs.

It was difficult to imagine that any living thing could survive such an attack. However, those of us who were aware of the story of Tarawa knew that the Japanese would emerge from their blockhouses and bunkers to kill and be killed on the beach on "D" day. Bitter experience had taught the Marines this lesson.

The 22nd was designated as Corps Reserve for the Kwajalien operation and as such did not participate in the assault landings. The United States Army's Seventh Division which had recently come down from Attu in the Aleutians made the landings on Kwajalien Island. The 4th Marine Division assaulted and captured the twin islands of Roi and Namur on the northern tip of the atoll. The reserve was not needed and we remained aboard ship watching the progress of the battle on the islands.

On February 3rd, the ships bearing the 22nd Regiment departed from Kwajalien atoll. We were told that we were to capture and secure Eniwetok atoll, a small group of islands to the north. There were three principal islands in the atoll; Engebi, Eniwetok and Parry Islands. We were to take them in that order. We arrived off Eniwetok on February 15th.

We had been aboard ship for almost 30 days with nothing to do but wait. We now had an objective. The troops suddenly became alive. Weapons were cleaned and oiled, packs were assembled and last minute letters were written. Anticipation – for what, we really did not know – but anticipation was rampant. Machine guns, mortars and radio and telephone communications equipment were dismantled, cleaned and reassembled. The ship was a beehive of activity.

"D" Day was set for February 18th and H hour was 9:30 P.M. Our officers briefed us from time to time on the progress of the campaign. We were assigned landing beaches, assault boats and time schedules for the attack. We were told what kind of resistance we might expect. Intelligence estimates of Japanese troop strength on each of the beaches was given to us. We were even told the percentage of casualties that we might expect among our units. This sort of information was never very comforting to me.

On the afternoon prior to the scheduled attack we were all issued hand grenades. I had received little prior training with grenades and I never felt safe with four of these deadly instruments hanging from my belt.

This was to be the first combat experience for the 22nd Marine Regiment. Anticipation was in the air. Despite the known dangers that would exist on the beach when dawn arrived tomorrow, there was a real desire among the men of the regiment to get in there and do what had to be done. I know now that ignorance of what we could encounter on that strip of sand was responsible for this feeling. After tomorrow we would no longer face a D-Day with such elation. It was my experience that veterans of previous battles were always less enthusiastic about a new battle than were green troops.

There was little sleep on board the <u>Leonard Wood</u> that night. My bunk was three decks down and the oppressive heat combined with the stench of about 300 unbathed bodies jammed into a space built for 100 men was not conducive to rest. Most of us spent the night on deck watching the low lying islands in the distance and speculating about the reception being planned for our arrival.

Those who managed to sleep were awakened at 4 o'clock by a simultaneous cacophony of reveille and a thunderous barrage of naval gunfire. This was the shelling of the beach which was to preceed our landing. The entire island seemed to be covered with exploding shells and soon a cloud of smoke hung over the atoll totally obscuring it from our view.

We were served a hot breakfast which we ate standing at tables built about chest high. There was not room to sit down and the standing arrangement made it possible to feed more troops at one time.

By 6:30 we had received final instructions and had descended the landing nets hung over the side of the ship into the LCVPs (landing craft vehicle and personnel). These were the famous Higgins boats of the Second World War. Most of them were fabricated in New Orleans. We were inside a lagoon and the sea was relatively calm. However, I always found that getting down the net into the landing craft without breaking a leg was an accomplishment to be long remembered. As the boats pulled away from the transport, the sailors on board leaned over the rail and wished us luck. It was at this point in a landing that I always wished that I had joined the Navy.

The landing boats moved away from the ship toward the island. Engebi was a small island and seemed to protrude only a few feet above the sea. The boats began to form circles. Each wave of boats formed a circle and idled lazily to await the signal to head for the beach. We could see planes flying low over the beach strafing the Japanese gun positions that were now beginning to fire at our boats. We began to see flashes of fire from the island and for the first time became aware of the fact that the war was not a one-sided affair. The Japanese were returning our fire.

Soon the first wave broke out of the circle, formed a line and headed for shore. We could see shells landing among the boats and tracers from shore based machine guns firing into the small boats as they headed for the beach. We watched the first and second waves proceed to the shore and soon it was our turn. The coxwain moved our boat into line and then we headed in. The Lieutenant in command stood in the front of the boat looking through a slit in the front ramp and gave us a description of the approaching island. We huddled in the doubtful security of the thin skinned craft. Shells were falling near our boats and I heard the Lieutenant say "Keep your head down. They are shooting at us now."

My greatest fear was that we would be hit before we could get off the boat or that we would be met by machine gun fire when the ramp was lowered and before we could disburse onto the beach and while we were still bunched in the boat. Neither of these fears materialized. About 100 yards from shore we were told to load our weapons and prepare to debark. The craft hit the beach, the ramp dropped and we were debarked onto the beach.

From the false security of the landing craft in which we huddled, we were suddenly thrown into what appeared to be utter turmoil. From the water's edge a sandy beach rose gradually for about thirty or forty yards to a slight rise or embankment over which we could not see. We rushed across the beach and fell into holes just beneath the high point of the rise. Guns were firing all around us. Marines were firing over the embankment out into the interior of the island. Other units were moving out off the beach and appeared to be attacking caves and bunkers which were about one hundred yards off the beach.

I thought, "God! I'm in the middle of a war and I'm not afraid." Somehow I thought I would be terrified. We all were concerned as to how we would react under fire. Like most, I was afraid, but not terrified and not too afraid to act. This was the important thing.

A strange smell hung over the beach. It was a vague, sweet, musty odor that we were to become familiar with in the months ahead. It was the odor of the Japanese Army and it was new and distinct. There are those who might question the fact that any particular race or nationality or ethnic group possesses an odor peculiar unto themselves. No Marine who fought the Japanese in the Pacific would debate this issue for long. He knew it to be a fact. The

Imperial Japanese Army possessed a peculiar odor. I never discovered the source of the smell. Perhaps it was the food that they ate, the oil or preservatives used on their weapons or their disinfectants. Whatever it was, it was there that February day in 1944 on the beach at Engebi. It mixed with the smell of burning gunpowder and cordite and the fumes of a hundred engines and the omnipresent smell of the dead, to create the odor of World War II as I knew it.

Our war had its own pungent odor. Twenty years later, as I examine Japanese books and uniforms that I brought back from the Pacific, the same odor, faint and sweet and musty arises to bring back vivid memories of those distant days. I have often wondered if Korea or Vietnam had such a distinctive perfume.

I was attached to Headquarters Company of the 3rd Battalion and as our unit formed we were ordered to move inland. We moved over the embankment and out onto a flat plain covered with shattered coconut trees and destroyed buildings and discarded equipment of all kinds. The island was covered with trenches, revetments and bunkers, all of which had been smashed and twisted by bombs and naval gunfire. Dead Japanese soldiers were everywhere. Some trenches would contain ten or fifteen dead soldiers, many blasted beyond recognition as human beings. I saw a body sitting against a tree with nothing visible above the waist but a bloody backbone protruding crazily toward a skull which had been blown off. It is perhaps not to the credit of man that we learned to accept this carnage so readily. Accept it we did, with an ease that was astounding. From that day forward we proceeded to the killing of the Japanese with no more emotion than had we been hunting rabbits back home. I say this with no pride. I am sure that the Japanese soldier had the same feeling.

As we moved inland I saw a dead Marine laying face down in a hole. This was something different. This I never learned to accept. This was ours. This could be me....in a few moments....tomorrow or the next week. Soldiers tend to ignore their dead. Somehow it was easier. I have seen an entire platoon walk past a dead Marine and never look at him. Perhaps this is survival psychology. I saw this reaction many times throughout the war. Someone always covered the face with a poncho or a helmet and somehow there was no personality left, only a body. This was not disrespect. It was a defense. When you have seen ten or twelve friends killed in one day it is beyond human capacity to dwell on the loss.

As we moved across the narrow island I saw more dead Marines. For the first time I became truly afraid. Always there was the knowledge that this could have been me.

Long after the war I read a book entitled <u>Beach Red</u>. The writer of this little volume came closer to explaining the real meaning of war than anyone that I have known. He wrote of war monuments. He said that he would not erect memorials of stone or granite to honor the war dead. The writer said:

"I would set aside a small plot of ground in the center of town as a memorial to war and I would dig ugly holes in the green grass and urinate upon it and defecate upon the ground and fill it with garbage and refuse and let it stink and smell in the hot summer sun and it would remind us of war." (Peter Bowman, <u>Beach Red</u>, 1945)

The writer knew and understood. He knew war as we knew it and he was right.

By the middle of the afternoon Japanese resistance was centered around the airstrip on the extreme northern tip of the island. The 22nd was slowly pushing the enemy into a pocket around the air field and eliminating them at a rapid rate. We established a command post near the center of the island and I was assigned the job of interrogating my first prisoners of war. I was taken to a large shell hole where four emaciated, half naked prisoners were squatting surrounded by Marine guards. I spoke to them in Japanese telling them that they would not be harmed. They answered and to my chagrin I could not understand a word of the reply. For one horrifying moment I feared that all of my language training had been for naught, when suddenly one prisoner spoke in Japanese almost as sophomoric as nine and explained in halting phrases that they were Koreans who had been pressed into labor battalions (Setsu Butai) in Korea by the Japanese Army and brought to the Pacific as labor troops. They were speaking Korean. I was to encounter these Koreans all over the Central Pacific. Though they were in fact not prisoners of war, I found them to be more sullen and troublesome than the Japanese. Most Japanese prisoners were cooperative, often friendly and very appreciative of kind treatment. They were apparently surprised that we did not mistreat them. They had been told of horrible atrocities committed by Marines at Guadalcanal and they expected the same treatment.

By late afternoon, the fighting was almost finished. Firing was sporadic and the forward elements of the 22nd Regiment were mopping up small pockets of resistance. We received orders to leave the island and to return to the transports in the lagoon. This was welcome news. The hot cramped and uncomfortable ship became a luxury liner when compared to the stinking island which was then knee deep in death and destruction.

As we formed, recovered our equipment and began to board the landing craft for the return trip, a Marine Defense Battalion was coming in ready to clean up the debris, bury the dead and begin the task of making the island habitable. Already the Seabees were at work on the airstrip to prepare it for use of American aircraft which were to attack the Marianas further west. On February 27th the Japanese airfield became operational as a Navy fighter strip.

Back aboard the <u>Leonard Wood</u> we were told that the 3rd Battalion was to serve as a reserve for the 106th Army Infantry Regiment which was to attack Eniwetok Island the next day.

The attack on February 19th against Eniwetok did not proceed as planned. The 106th Army Infantry was not equal to the task of overcoming the cleverly entrenched Japanese. The 3rd Battalion of the 22nd Marines was ordered ashore during the afternoon to assist the attack. Again we assembled our gear, were issued ammunition and went over the side of the ship into the landing boats and headed for the beach.

The procedure was the same. Each wave formed a lazy circle a few thousand yards off the beach. As the proper signal was given from the shore, each circle broke out into a single line and headed toward the beach. We were in the third wave going in. The landing areas were secure. However, soldiers were still crouched in fox holes along the beach. We proceeded through their lines into the interior of the island where we turned right and commenced an attack toward the south end of the island. Eniwetok Island was different from most of the islands in the atoll. It was heavily wooded. In some areas the foliage under the palm trees was dense and thick. The enemy was difficult to find. By the time that our line was established night had fallen. In the Pacific campaigns fighting and movement generally ceased at dusk. Objects moving at night, whether friend or foe, were shot. We were told to dig in for the night.

Battalion Headquarters to which I was attached bedded down in a small clearing. We dug foxholes under palm trees which towered above us. This was to be our first night under fire. As I finished my hole which permitted me to get my body about five inches beneath the surface of the ground, I could hear firing from a position about 100 yards to our front.

We were now beginning to acquire combat experience. We soon learned that sound was as important as sight. The Japanese light machine gun (Nambu) was a fast firing weapon with a high pitched sound. It was easily distinguished from our own .30 caliber machine gun with its slower pace or our .50 caliber weapon with its deep rasp. At this time our position must have been only a few hundred feet from the beach as I could hear the surf pounding during the night.

Destroyers were patrolling the southern end of the island during the night and periodically they fired parachute flares high into the sky. This was apparently an effort to prevent Japanese surprise attacks. As the flares fell slowly back to earth they illuminated the surrounding jungle with a ghostly light. I hated the flares. They seemed to dispel the protective cloak of darkness and to encourage the enemy to look for us. The night was long and terrible. Machine guns fired during the night and tracer bullets were fired over our heads. We stayed as close to the earth as we could. I could hear Marines shouting and occasionally an answer in Japanese.

With the first light of dawn the troops began to move about. Scarcely had the movement began when the Japanese launched an attack upon the Command Post. An enemy platoon had infiltrated the area during the night and was attacking from the direction of the sea. Guns began to fire all around us. The Marines on guard duty around the Command Post were heavily engaged.

I was lying on my back in the foxhole and I could feel bullets five feet over my head ripping into the dense foliage scattering leaves and debris down upon me. I had not trained with this outfit and I had never been told what my duties were in such cases as this. Looking over the edge of my hole, I could see Marines moving forward toward the sea. I could see Japanese soldiers running back away from the area. During all of this time heavy gunfire reverberated through the jungle around us. Occasionally the blast of a hand grenade or a dynamite charge could be heard as our troops moved up to defend the Command Post.

The action ceased almost as rapidly as it had started. It had lasted about fifteen minutes. I had not fired a shot. I had seen the enemy but our troops had been between my position and the Japanese. Two men of our headquarters unit were killed in the action not far from where I lay in a foxhole. Both of them had bunked near me on the ship. Their bodies were wrapped in ponchos and brought back to the Command Post.

A Japanese soldier had been killed near a jeep that was parked about fifty feet from my hole. I went over to look at him. He was smaller than I had imagined the enemy to be. He did not look very formidable. He looked like a rag doll all twisted out of shape end covered with blood. I was also told that our Battalion Surgeon had been stabbed with a bayonet during the night and had been sent back to a hospital. Ten Marines including the Battalion Operations Officer were killed in the attack.

Shortly after the attack on the Command Post I was ordered to accompany three Marine guards who were to take six prisoners out to a ship in the lagoon. The prisoners had been captured during the early morning fight. With the prisoners in tow we went back to the beach and boarded a landing craft which took us to a ship in the lagoon.

As we boarded the vessel sailors and navy personnel crowded around us. This was their first glimpse of war at close range. We were dirty, stained with the filth of battle standing on the deck of a warship flying an Admiral's flag. We were strangely out of place. We were treated with great deference as if we had returned from some strange adventure as heroes. The sailors offered us food and cigarettes.

I was told to accompany a Marine guard dressed in a clean pressed khaki uniform. I told the prisoners that they would be treated well - "Daijobu Desu" - and followed the guard into the interior of the ship.

We went to a room containing long tables covered with maps. There were a number of officers apparently expecting us. The guard told the officers that I had just come aboard from the island. I recognized an Admiral by his stars. He asked me how things were going on the beach. I told him what I knew of the progress of the battle. He inquired about the morale of the troops. He asked me if I had interrogated any Japanese prisoners. I made my report—Corporal to Admiral. I never knew his name. I always believed that the Admiral was Harry Hill, the Task Force Commander.

The interview ended. Admirals do not converse very long with Corporals. "Get this lad something to eat" the Admiral said, "and send him back to the beach."

I was taken to the galley and given warm food. The sailors asked, "How is it on the island?" They were interested in souvenirs – battle flags and Japanese insignia. I had none. Next time I would come prepared to barter.

After the meal I rejoined the Marine guards on the deck of the ship. I could see the island in the distance. Planes were bombing the southern tip into which the enemy had been pressed. Smoke shrouded most of the trees which were visible from the ship. The ship was safe and clean. I did not want to go back. I remembered the terrible night before and wondered if I would spend another such night crouched in a foxhole on an island that smelled of death and turmoil. Soon a landing craft pulled alongside and we descended a ladder into the boat which immediately pulled away and headed for Eniwetok. The sailors wished us well as we departed. They always did this. It was a ritual. It was also sincere.

I rejoined the 3rd Battalion as it continued to attack the remaining enemy troops on the island. We moved forward establishing our Command Post a hundred yards or so back of the forward platoons. Enemy dead were no longer an oddity. There were too many of them. We searched some of them removing dog-tags, diaries, letters and photographs from pockets and packs. Occasionally Corpsmen passed with wounded Marines on stretchers. Dead Marines were brought back to the Command Post and laid out side by side.

I interrogated several prisoners asking questions requested by the Battalion Intelligence Officer. My Japanese was adequate and I was pleased that I could converse with the prisoners. At a captured headquarters bunker, I was asked to identify documents and to separate military orders and papers from those of a more personal nature. This I was able to do without a great deal of difficulty. My limited knowledge of the written Japanese was sufficient for me to perform this task. Even though I could not read many of the documents I was able to identify them.

By late afternoon organized resistance had ended. Our Battalion was withdrawn from the island leaving the army to completely secure the area. We returned to the <u>Leonard Wood.</u>

The Navy had coffee and sandwiches awaiting us in the mess. We proceeded to chow before the luxury of a saltwater shower. While we ate at tables standing up in the mess hall of the <u>Leonard Wood</u>, one of the most famous photographs of World War II was made. A copy of this photograph is attached to this memoir. It is a picture of three Marines of the 22nd Regiment on board our ship after spending two days and one night in battle on Eniwetok Island. This is how we looked when we returned to the ship. This is the aftermath of battle. This is what we were – what we had become. It was a long way from the campus of Louisiana State University which I had left only one year earlier.

I was nineteen years old on the day we attacked Eniwetok.

After chow and showers the men of the Third Battalion of the 22nd Regiment of Marines headed for a well-earned rest in their bunks. We were secure in the knowledge that we had at last met the Gods of War on their own ground and had survived. Two assault landings against heavily fortified islands and four days of constant fighting seemed to indicate a rest. Such was not to be.

One island in the atoll remained in Japanese hands. Parry Island is shaped like a large raindrop about 2,000 yards long and about 500 yards across at its widest part. The Japanese had built two major defense works on the northwest side of the island. Enemy troops on Parry numbered about 1,350 as compared to 850 on Eniwetok.

Marine General Thomas E. Watson, the troop commander for the operation, was not satisfied with the performance of the Army troops on Eniwetok and despite the fact that the Marines had done most of the fighting he decided that he must use them to attack Parry. The troops of the First and Second Battalions were brought down from Engebi to join the Third Battalion in the attack on Parry which was scheduled for 9:00 o'clock A.M., February 22nd.

In mid-afternoon of February 21, we of the Third Battalion were informed that at dawn of the next day we would again be expected to assault another island and wrest its control from a determined enemy who would kill and maim a number of us in the process. The war began to look like a dead-end street. Every tomorrow was a yesterday. The only thing that mattered was survival. I looked at the two empty bunks across from me and wondered.

I was now afraid — really afraid for the very first time. Now I knew what was on those islands. I knew what a .31 caliber bullet could do to a man's stomach or to his face. I knew how a human body looked when after death it cooked in the tropical sun for three days. And worse, I knew how it smelled and how many flies it attracted. I knew how a hundred bodies looked and smelled. If these honored dead were heroes, either American or Japanese, there was no dignity to their death.

All of the glory and honor of man, all of the beauty and intellectual accomplishments of civilization were reduced to nothingness – to absurdity – on those small strips of sand in that vast Ocean. Man, that fortunate creature that God so richly endowed, killing man. It was obscene. From that day, I hated guns. For twenty-one more months I carried one daily and eventually used it to kill. This was necessary to survive. At the end, I gave my rifle back to the Corps from whence it came and never again desired to use one.

Often during the last twenty years at cocktail parties or at fancy restaurants or in comfortable homes, I hear a well-dressed bon vivant say "Why don't we send in the Marines and clean them out?" — "Bomb 'em back to the Stone Age." I make no moral judgments. I make no political decisions. I just remember the beach at Eniwetok. I don't want to go back. I don't want my children to go back. I wonder if he was ever there, this sender of Marines, if he ever smelled the dead, cooking, rotting in the hot sand of a nameless tropical island.

I remember less of the affair at Parry Island than of any action in which I participated. On the evening of February 21st we again were issued live ammunition and grenades. We cleaned and repaired equipment and slept very little that night. The Navy began early on the following morning to bombard the Island. The roar of guns and the flashes of fire awakened us to the fact that we were next on the agenda.

The procedure for attack was now well known to all of us. Over the side of the ship and down the nets into the landing craft and a long wait in a bouncing Higgins boat before receiving the signal to head into the beach. The Third Battalion was ordered in at 10:00 o'clock in the morning.

I was assigned to a boat that carried a squad armed with flamethrowers. A flamethrower consists of two metal tanks welded together which fit in a device strapped to the back of a Marine. One tank contains oxygen and the other the chemical that produces the flame and furnishes the body for its delivery toward the enemy. Several of these flamethrowers were stored in the middle of our boat leaning against seven or eight boxes of hand grenades that were being transported to the beach.

While our Higgins boat was moving around the circle awaiting orders to head for the island, a wave struck us rather sharply causing a box of hand grenades to fall several feet onto the bottom of the boat. I immediately heard the sharp hissing sound that the fuse of a grenade emits just before it explodes. Believing that a grenade was about to explode in the middle of a boat carrying seven boxes of grenades and tanks of fuel for flamethrowers, three Marines including myself dived over the side into the sea to escape. I dove as far from the boat as I was able and swam underwater for as long as I could hold my breath awaiting every second to hear and feel the explosion that would rip our boat apart and wondering what it would do to me. When I could hold my breath no longer I swam to the surface and saw our boat still intact and coming around to pick us up. I was pulled into the boat dripping wet and minus my rifle which had dropped into the water when I left the boat. What we imagined to be the sound of a grenade fuse was a jet on a flamethrower that had been jarred open by the falling box and was allowing oxygen to escape. I was glad to be alive but humiliated before the troops who had remained in the landing craft. The reaction of our peers was a study in compassion and understanding. The actions of the three who jumped from the boat was thought to have been so plausible in view of the evidence that we were almost admired for our quick thinking. I was, however, faced with the prospect of being deposited onto an enemy held island minus a weapon for defense.

Shortly after being pulled back into the boat we received orders to head for the landing beaches. The Lieutenant in charge of our boat told me to pick up a weapon from a wounded Marine as soon as we hit the beach. We struck the beach at about 10:00 o'clock. The ramp of the boat dropped and we rushed out onto the beach wading through the surf for about twenty-five yards and viewing almost the identical scene that we had previously witnessed at Engebi and on Eniwetok. The devastation on Parry was complete. No structures remained intact above ground level. Trenches, bunkers and buildings were simply obliterated. Japanese dead were everywhere. Naval gunfire is a terrible affliction. In later years pictures of the barren landscape of the moon would remind me of these islands.

I had only been on the island a few minutes when I found a carbine near a dead Marine. I took the carbine together with several clips of ammunition from his belt. I carried this weapon with me throughout the remaining months of the war. When it came time to give it back to the Marine Corps, I had a difficult time explaining the fact that I was not returning the same weapon that had been issued to me at boot camp two years before. I liked the carbine. It was a .30 caliber weapon that was much lighter than the M-1 rifle that I had previously used. It was better for the type of work that I was doing. It was a fast firing weapon and the ammunition for it was lighter than that required for the M-1.

Parry was vigorously defended. If we took any prisoners I did not see them. We must have killed every enemy soldier on the island. The Japanese did not often surrender. The <u>Bushido</u> – code of the Samurai – indicated that death was to be preferred to surrender.

The island was like a prairie-dog town. The underground shelters were like spiderwebs. The enemy could move from one bunker to another by means of tunnels. A bunker would be blown up and bypassed by Marines who would then be fired upon by Japanese in the rear who had escaped the bunker and moved underground to another strong point.

For the first time I saw tanks and flamethrowers in action. I saw enemy soldiers run from pillboxes only to be burned to a crisp by the searching tongues of flame that spewed from the nozzle of a flamethrower. Of all the horrors of war this, together with napalm bombs was the most terrible. The human body does not burn very well. The outside skin bums easily, but the body liquids beneath retard the effect and often only sizzles and smells.

For the first time, I fired my weapon. Often we fired at sounds, at movements which were suspect. At trees, at bunkers and into holes in the ground. Sometimes we shot at wounded soldiers who had been bypassed and left for dead, but who hid and fired at us from the rear after we had passed. I saw several Marines hit by this type of fire. I saw dead Marines often with a rifle stuck in the sand beside them to mark the body for burial parties.

Shortly after the landing the Third Battalion joined the Second and began to drive to the north end of the island. We overran and captured the headquarters of Major General Yoshima Nishida, the Atoll Commander. General Nishida had only arrived at Eniwetok on January 4th with 3000 troops of the First Amphibious Brigade. This was a veteran unit of tough, experienced soldiers. I spent part of the day examining field orders and other documents found in the headquarters files. I found the General's personal photograph album. I have his picture taken from the album as well as his calling card which properly identified him as "Major General Yoshima Nishida, Commander 3130 Brigade." We never did find the General.

By late afternoon the remaining Japanese had been driven toward the southern tip of the island. The advancing Marines formed a skirmish line across the narrow island and with tanks and flamethrowers leading the way began to push the enemy into the sea and kill them at a rapid rate. The Marines suffered heavy casualties in some areas of thick foliage. By 7:30 in the evening we reached the end of the island and dug in for the night.

Again we spent a long night crouched in foxholes a few yards behind the advance platoons. Destroyers kept the island lighted all night with search lights and parachute flares. All through the night the Japanese tried to launch counter-attacks but they were quickly destroyed and broken up.

When morning came most of the enemy had been killed or had killed themselves during the night. Shortly before noon we were told to collect our gear and move back to the beach to prepare for transport to the Leonard Wood. The troops of the third Battalion of the 106th Army Infantry came in to take up garrison duty.

We headed back to the beach, boarded the small landing ships and went back to the security of the ship. At last it was finished. Operation Catchpole, the code name for the Eniwetok operation, was complete. The troops were quiet. Most of us ate, cleaned up and went to sleep. For the rest of our lives we would remember the last seven days. There was time enough for storytelling. That night we slept.

We had killed 3,400 Japanese soldiers who died in a futile defense of the Atoll at a cost of 254 Marines killed and 555 wounded. Army units lost 94 killed and 311 wounded. Of the dead Marines four bunked near me on the Leonard Wood. As an amphibious operation Catchpole was classic. The 22nd Marines had performed well. Mistakes had been made but overall results were excellent. The enemy was vanquished in record time. It was time to move on.

The defenses of the Marshall Islands were shattered. The powerful Japanese bases in the Western Marshalls at Mille, Jaluit, Wotje and Maleolap were bypassed and neutralized for the remainder of the war. With Eniwetok Atoll under American control the Japanese were not capable of supplying or reinforcing those Marshall bases over which the Japanese flag still flew. Thousands of Japanese soldiers were rendered useless. Before I left Engebi American engineers were already beginning to construct airfields from which our planes could fly to attack enemy installations in the Marianas Islands. American submarines could now operate from bases closer to the sea-lanes over which war materials were shipped from conquered territories to Japanese industrial centers. One more step was complete on the road to Tokyo. The Marshall Islands which had been entrusted to Japan by the League of Nations after World War I were now firmly under American control.

The scuttlebutt was that we would be sent to Guadalcanal for rest and training. That seemed agreeable to the troops. We could land on Guadalcanal without the necessity of killing its present inhabitants. It had been pacified many months before. We could expect a friendly greeting upon arrival.

Early the next morning an announcement over the ship's speaker ordered me to report to Battalion Headquarters. Upon arrival at that office, I was told that I was being transferred to the U.S.S. President Coolidge for transport back to Pearl Harbor along with other specialized personnel who had been temporarily assigned to the 22nd Regiment for the Catchpole operation. I knew that this was wrong. I told Gunnery Sergeant Nagazine that I had been assigned permanently to the 22nd and that I had brought my record book and staff returns with me when I first reported to him. No amount of argument could change his mind. It was assumed that I had been temporarily assigned as an interpreter and that I should now go back to Fifth Amphibious Corps Headquarters at Pearl Harbor. I was told to pack my bag, get my rifle and get my ass out of his sight. I did just that. It is not wise to argue with a Marine Gunnery Sergeant. I was not lacking in such wisdom. I was told that formal orders would be sent to me later as records were then stored in the hold of the ship.

Along with other specially trained troops including several language officers that I had briefly met before, I was transferred from the Leonard Wood to the U.S. President Coolidge. Two days later we put to sea, passed out of the lagoon and headed for Pearl Harbor. As I watched Eniwetok fade into the distance, I knew that those islands would always remain with me. The memories of those last few days would forever color and influence my thoughts. The passage of years takes its toll on the accuracy of memory.

It is not easy to remember what one thought at age nineteen. I was glad to be alive. I was glad to be leaving that place. I wanted to go home. I wanted to see those that I loved. I wanted to read their letters and to know that they cared for me. I wanted to go to a quiet place where there were no guns, no explosives, no flares in the night and no odor of burning flesh.

I never wanted to go back. I knew that someday I would. There would be other islands and other battles.

CHAPTER 4

Hawaii Revisited

WE WERE TWO DAYS OUT of Eniwetok when I fully realized my rather precarious position. Marines do not move from one place to another without orders which specify a destination, a time of arrival and a person to whom to report. I had none of these. Gunnery Sergeant Nagazine said to go and I went. Most of the enlisted troops aboard the U.S.S. President Coolidge were attached to small groups such as an independent scout platoon, a detached communications unit or a special hospital unit. These people had officers and a destination. I had none. The trip back was like a vacation. I had no duties. I did not know what I would do when we arrived at Pearl Harbor.

After about fifteen days at sea we arrived at Pearl Harbor during the middle of March. As the ship pulled alongside the pier a band was playing and there was a small crowd to welcome the returning troops. I picked up my seabag and my rifle and went to the forward deck. As an officer called each unit by name, the troops attached would depart down the gangplank. They were greeted by cheers and by girls in native costume, who placed leis of flowers around their necks usually accompanied by a kiss. The troops boarded waiting trucks and were driven off.

After about an hour all of the troops had left, the band had departed and the girls were gone. I was left alone on the deck. I picked up my gear and walked down the gangplank to the pier below. The pier was deserted except for a single jeep parked near a small guardhouse. I walked over to the jeep and was surprised to find that the driver was a Marine whom I had known from my duty at Camp Linda Vista. I told him my story. He asked what I wanted to do. I said that I should probably go back to the officer who had first sent me off to war. The jeep driver agreed to take me to Headquarters of the Fifth Amphibious Corps at Camp Catlin.

At Camp Catlin I again walked into the office of Warrant Officer S.A. Guy. I told him my story. His reply was a profane classic. I had indeed been assigned permanently to the 22nd Marines and I "damn well better get my ass back to them in a hurry." The Marine Corps always seemed to take an inordinate amount of interest in the geographical location of my ass. Considering the fact that the 22nd Marines were on Guadalcanal four thousand miles away, it was agreed that I required some assistance. I was sent back to the Transient Center with orders to go back to the 22nd Marines with the first replacements sent to them from the Center.

A description of the Transient Center was given in a previous chapter. It was the Camp to which I had been assigned when I first arrived at Pearl Harbor two months earlier. I was posted to a tent, given the location of a mess hall at which I could eat and told to report to the center's office three times each day to catch a boat to Guadalcanal when one was available.

I was still an orphan. I knew no one and no one seemed to know me. I had no permanent address and consequently received no mail. I had received no letters from home since leaving the states more than two months before. I finally discovered a way to sneak through a pineapple field and get into the adjacent Camp Catlin from the rear. I located Kirby Darden, my fellow graduate of the Japanese Language School, and for the first time since we shipped out, I felt at home. By using Kirby's address I managed to receive a few letters from my mother.

I possessed one virtue at this stage of my service that made my life easier. This I had acquired on the beaches at Eniwetok. I was now a veteran. This distinguished me from ninety per cent of the troops in the camp. I had seen the War. Where they were going, I had already been. All of the things that they had been trained to do, I had presumably done. I had earned my stripes. Battle experience lent great prestige to one in this environment. It mattered not if you had won a decoration, slain the enemy or destroyed a pillbox single handedly. Just having been there was sufficient. It made one a bit taller, a bit tougher, more worldly — a little saltier. We all reaped the harvest of this experience. Every night the newly arrived Marines gathered in my tent to talk about the fighting and view the Japanese dog tags, insignia and other trophies that I had brought back from Eniwetok.

"What was it like?" they asked. Surely my answers did nothing to prepare them for their later experiences on the beaches of Saipan, Iwo Jima or Okinawa. Nothing could have done that.

Somehow I missed the boat for Guadalcanal and the 22nd Marines. I never did know why this happened. I was called in one day in early April, 1944 and given orders to report to Headquarters Company, First Base Headquarters Battalion, Fleet Marine Force which was then being formed at the Transient Center. By this time moving was no problem. I packed my bag, picked up my carbine and took a jeep to my new assignment. I was happy. At least someone wanted me. I was leaving the orphanage.

THE SHREVEPORT TIMES,

Shreveport Marine Can Talk Back to 'Em Now

Corp. Allen Jerry Tillery, 18, left, graduated recently from the Japanese language school at the marine corps training center in Camp Elliott, Calif. Tillery was highest ranking student in his class.

A 1941 graduate of Fair Park high school, he was lieutenant-colonel of the R.O.T.C. battalion there and attended Louisiana State university for a semester. He entered the marines in April and has now been assigned to the headquarters company of an amphibious corps which will see active duty after more training.

In the language school, under the direction of Capt. F. O. Wolf, who questioned one of the first Jap prisoners captured on Guadalcanal, Tillery took a 98-day course after meeting rigid qualifications. He mastered Japanese military terminology, written and spoken and will be sent into the field as a combat interpreter.

His parents are Mr. and Mrs. James H. Tillery, 286 Quinton street. His brother, Jim Tillery, was with Carlson's Marine Raiders when they landed at Makin island recently.

Shreveport Times, 1943

News About Those in The Military Services

Our News About Those in the Military Services column is dedicated to the boys of Shreveport and vicinity and their families. If any of your sons, friends and relatives have won promotion, are home on leave, overseas, or have been transferred to a new base, please contact us, either by mail, telephone, or come up to the editorial room of The Journal. We like to use pictures and information of the boys, so please send us as much news about the service men as is possible.

Camp Elliott, San Diego, Cal.—Pfc. ALLEN J. TILLERY, son of Mr. and Mrs. James H. Tillery, who live at 2601 Quinton street, Shreveport, La., has been graduated from the Japanese language school at the marine corps training center, Camp Elliott, Cal.

The language school, under the direction of Capt. F. O. Wolf, who has the distinction of having questioned one of the first Japanese prisoners captured on Guadalcanal, offers a 90-day course to enlisted men who meet the rigid qualifications. The course is taught purely for the business at hand with the main efforts of the students being directed toward the mastering of Japanese military terminology, written and spoken.

Private First-Class Tillery will be advanced to corporal and sent into the field as a combat interpreter.

Shreveport Times, 1943

Corporal Allen J. Tillery (standing, 4th from right) with his unit on Tinian, 1944

Temporary graves for some of the 326 of the 2nd and 4th U.S. Marine
Divisions, V Amphibious Corps who liberated Tinian, 1944

Corporal Allen J. Tillery (hand on helmet, center) translates as a
young Japanese "soldier" surrenders to Tillery's Lieutenant

Corporal Allen J. Tillery's unit, G-2 Section, First Base Headquarters Battalion, Tinian seeing off their commander Col. Clyde H. Metcalf, U.S.M.C., 1944 who was retiring; Lt. Colonel Metcalf had been Chief of the Historical Section of the U.S. Marine Corps and author of <u>A History of the U.S. Marine Corps</u> (G.P. Putnam's Sons 1939)

Japanese long range artillery emplacement hidden in cave on Tinian, 1944

U.S. Marines taking in stride flooding of their camp, Tinian 1944

U.S. Marines pause to pray for peace while their band of brothers
continue the fight in the distance, Tinian, 1944

Japanese long-range 150 mm artillery emplacement which menaced
the U.S. Tinian invasion fleet, July 16 – August 1, 1944

Remnants of Tinian Town, Tinian after naval bombardment by U.S.
Navy, 3 battleships, 5 cruisers and 16 destroyers, August 2, 1944

U.S. Marines at the ruins of two megalithic columns near the beach of Tinian
Town, Tinian 1944, said to be ruins of honorary crypts of a Chamorro
Chief, Taga, now an archaeological site known as House of Taga

Enlisted Marines in School and at War

Allen J. Tillery and Calvin W. Dunbar standing outside their *nipa* hut at the POW prison camp on Guam in 1945. *Roger Pineau Collection,* Box 11-Folder 2, University of Colorado at Boulder Libraries.

Corporal Allen J. Tillery, U.S.M.C. and Corporal Calvin W. Dunbar, U.S.M.C. outside their "nipa" hut at the POW prison camp on Guam in 1945. Roger Pineau Collection, Box 11, Folder 2, University of Colorado at Boulder Libraries. From Kanji & Codes – Learning Japanese for World War II, Irwin L. and Cole E. Slesnick (2006), p. 205

RESERVE 841175 FILE

DURATION OF NATIONAL EMERGENCY

TILLERY

Allen Jere

BORN: 31 January 1925

AT: Shreveport, La.

ENLISTED: 24 April 1943
Accepted: Shreveport, La.
New Orleans, La.

AT:

24 Apr 43 - 24 Apr 43 - USMC- SS
Rec. Depot, San Diego   Cl 3c
TEMPORARY   Cl 3b

PVT 1st CLASS   LINE   JUL 2 1943

Jd 7th Recruit Bn, Recruit Depot.   APR 7 1943

TEMPORARY
CORPORAL   LINE   NOV 4 1943

Jd Hq&Ser Co School Bn,
Trng. Center, Camp Elliott, Cal.   JUL 3 1943

Jd. Co. B   NOV 8 1943
Casual Bn.   Camp Elliott, Calif
Hq. & Serv. Bn.
5th. Amphs. Corps

Jd Rear Echelon 5th. Amphs. Corps NOV 10 1943

In The Field Via "Manila Bay" JAN 3 1944

Jd. Hq & Ser Co 22nd Marines FMF ILN 13 1944

Jd. Hq.Co. Hq. & Serv. Bn.   JAN 9 1944
5th. Amphs. Corps.

Jd. Replacement Bn,   MAR 8 1944
Transient Ctr 5th. Amphs. Corps.

Desig. Chgd to Transient Ctr. 5th Amphs Corps

Repln Bn Mar. Adm. Comd.   MAY 8 1944

Jd Re.Co. 2nd Prov.BaseHq Bn   JUN 5 1944

Jd. Hd Co. 1st Base Hq Bn   MAR 17 1945

From In The Field Via   AUG 16 1945
USS Joseph T. Dickman

Jd. Off App Bn Schools Regt.   AUG 27 19
TrngComd FMF Camp Lejeune, N.C.

12th Processing Co. Re-DistbnBn
Jd Redistbn&Repln Regt   SEP 10 1945

Designation changed to 12th Processing Co.
Re-DistbnBn Redistbn&Repln Regt   SEP 15 1945

Honorable Dis   Corp

OCT. 1 1945

12th ProcessingCo
Re-DistbnBn
R & R Regt.
Camp LeJeune, N. C.

FILE

Corporal Allen J. Tillery's Official U.S. Marine Corps Record of Service #841175. Enlisted: April 24, 1943 – Honorable Discharge, October 1, 1945

U. S. MARINE CORPS REPORT OF SEPARATION

NAVMC 78-PD.

CODE COLUMN

1. LAST NAME	FIRST NAME	MIDDLE NAMES	2. RANK	3. PAY GRADE	4. SERIAL NUMBER
TILLERY	ALLEN	JERE	CORP	65	841175

5. PERMANENT ADDRESS FOR MAILING PURPOSES: 2716 Penick St, Shreveport, La.

6. RACE	7. SEX	8. CITIZEN	9. DATE OF BIRTH
W	M	YES NO	31 Jan 25

10. ADDRESS FROM WHICH PERSON WILL SEEK EMPLOYMENT: 2716 Penick St, Shreveport, La.

11. MARRIED	12. NO. OF DEP.	13. PLACE OF BIRTH
YES NO	none	Shreveport, La.

RECORD OF MARINE CORPS SERVICE

SELECTIVE SERVICE DATA

14. REGISTERED	15. ADDRESS AT TIME OF ENTRY INTO SERVICE	16. SEL. SER. BD. NO.	17. COUNTY & STATE
YES NO	2601 Quinton St, Shreveport, La.	2	Caddo Co, La.

18. MEANS OF ENTRY			19. PLACE OF ENTRY INTO ACTIVE SERVICE	20. DATE OF ENTRY	21. COMPONENT
ENLISTED	INDUCTED	COMMISSIONED	New Orleans, La.	24 Apr 43	REG. III
X	I				

22. PENSION CLAIM FILED	23. PLACE OF SEPARATION FROM ACTIVE SERVICE	24. DATE OF SEPARATION	25. ORG. AT SEPARATION
YES NO X	Camp Lejeune, N.C.	10 Oct 45	Rad Bn.

26. TYPE OF DISCHARGE CERT.	27. LENGTH OF FOREIGN AND/OR SEA SERVICE	YEARS	MOS.	DYS.
HONORABLE		1	7	14

28. MILITARY SPECIALTIES: Translator(Jap) 267

29. SERVICE SCHOOLS ATTENDED	COURSES	WEEKS
Jap language school, Camp Elliott, Cal.	Translator	12

30. PRINCIPAL MILITARY DUTY: Translator(Jap) 267

EMPLOYMENT AND NON-SERVICE EDUCATIONAL DATA

31. CIVILIAN OCCUPATION (TITLE)	D.O.T. NUMBER	NO. YRS.	LAST EMPLOYED
Student, high school	O-x		

JOB SUMMARY

32. SECONDARY OCCUPATION (TITLE)	D.O.T. NUMBER	NO. YRS.	LAST EMPLOYED

33. LAST EMPLOYER BEFORE ENTRY INTO SERVICE	DATE LEFT	34. JOB AID DESIRED
		YES NO X

35. EDUCATION IN YEARS

GRAMMAR	HIGH SCHOOL	COLLEGE	DEGREE	36. MAJOR COURSES
8	4	6/12		Academic

37. TRADE COURSES	38. COURSES OF GREATEST INTEREST	39. LAST SCHOOL ATTENDED
		La. State U, Baton Rouge, La.

PREFERENCES

40. PREFERENCE FOR ADDITIONAL TRAINING: complete college training

41. JOB PREFERENCE	REASON
none desired	will devote full time to education

42. LOCALITY PREFERENCE	REASON
undecided	

I certify that all information on this form pertaining to the Naval Service of the above named individual is in accordance with the records of the U. S. Marine Corps and that a copy of this form has been delivered to him in person.

43. *F L Dixon Jr*
SIGNATURE OF C.O. OR PERS.O.

F. L. DIXON JR., 2nd Lt., USMCR
TYPE IN NAME OF OFF. - RANK

Allen J Tillery
SIGNATURE OF DISCHARGEE   DATE 24 Sep 45

TO. HEADQUARTERS MARINE CORPS   REDIFORM—PATD.—AMERICAN SALES BOOK CO., INC., NIAGARA FALLS, N.Y.

Corporal Allen J. Tillery's U.S. Marine Corps Report
of Separation, September 24, 1945

PROFESSIONAL AND CONDUCT RECORD OF   TILLERY, Allen Jere

Headquarters Company, Second Provisional Base Headquarters Battalion, Fifth
Amphibious Corps, C/O Fleet Post Office, San Francisco, California. Redesig-
nated: Headquarters Company, Second Base Headquarters Battalion, Fleet
Marine Forces, Pacific C/O Fleet Post Office, San Francisco, Calif., by Island
Command Special Order 31-44 dtd 27Au-44. Auth: U.S. Naval Dispatch fr CG, FMF
Pac, 260126, dtd 25Aug44.

HEADQUARTERS COMPANY,
SECOND BASE HEADQUARTERS BATTALION,
FLEET MARINE FORCE, PACIFIC,
C/O FLEET POST OFFICE,
SAN FRANCISCO, CALIFORNIA.

23 February, 1945.

A-F-F-I-D-A-V-I-T

I TILLERY, Allen J., a Corporal in the U. S. Marine Corps(Reserve),
do solemnly swear or affirm that the information contained herein is true to
the best of my knowledge and belief.

13 January, 1944, embarked aboard USS PRESIDENT MONROE at P.H., Oahu, T.H.,
and sailed therefrom 14, 15, arr at Maui, T.H., and debarked thereat. 16
January, 1944 embarked aboard USS PRESIDENT MONROE at Maui, T.H., 17, sailed
therefrom; 18, arr at P. H., Oahu, T.H., and debarked thereat.

20 January, 1944, embarked aboard USS LEONARD WOOD at P.H., Oahu, T.H., and
sailed therefrom; 20-29 January, underway enroute Marshall Islands. 30-31,
January, 1944-14 February, 1944, berthed thereat; 15 February, 1944, sailed
therefrom and underway enroute Enewetok, Atoll, 17-20 February, 1944,
participated in the Capture of Engebi, Enewetok, and Parry Islands, Enewetok
Atoll. 22-23 February, 1944 enroute; 24 February, 1944, disembarked at
Roi, Kwajalein, Atoll. 25 February, 1944, embarked aboard USS NEVILLE at Roi
Island; 26, sailed therefrom 8 March,1944, arr at P.H., Oahu, T.H., and
debarked thereat.

ALLEN J. TILLERY

Sworn to before me this 23 February, 1945.

BRUCE J. BROADY, JR.
Capt., USMCR.
CO, HqCo.

61

Embarked aboard the U. S. S. MANILLA BAY, at San Diego, California
on 2 January, 1944. Disembarked at Pearl Harbor, T.H., 9 January,
1944. 4 Busiled

EARLE G. DUNN, 1stLt., USMCR.

MEDALS (including good-conduct medals and bars, but excluding those awarded for qualification with infantry weapons), BADGES, AND DECORATIONS; MEDAL OR BADGE NUMBER AND DATE AWARDED

LETTERS OF COMMENDATION (Pasted on page 23)

Subject	Date	By Whom Issued
Forld with G-2 Intelligence patrol - see page -19	5 Feb. 45	Brig Gen V. H. Kimble

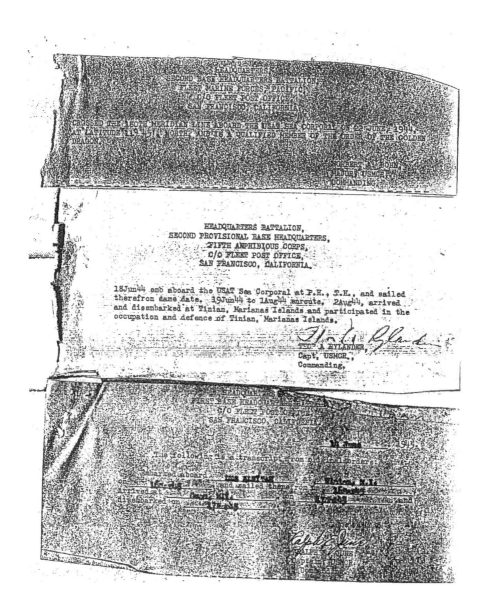

HEADQUARTERS
SECOND BASE HEADQUARTERS BATTALION,
FLEET MARINE FORCES, PACIFIC,
C/O FLEET POST OFFICE,
SAN FRANCISCO, CALIFORNIA

CROSSED THE 180TH MERIDIAN LINE ABOARD THE USAT SEA CORPORAL ON 22 JUNE 1944, AT LATITUDE 11° 17' NORTH, AND IS A QUALIFIED MEMBER OF THE ORDER OF THE GOLDEN DRAGON.

ROBERT E. BORN,
MAJOR, USMCR,
COMMANDING.

HEADQUARTERS BATTALION,
SECOND PROVISIONAL BASE HEADQUARTERS,
FIFTH AMPHIBIOUS CORPS,
C/O FLEET POST OFFICE,
SAN FRANCISCO, CALIFORNIA.

18Jun44 emb aboard the USAT Sea Corporal at P.H., T.H., and sailed therefrom same date. 19Jun44 to 1Aug44 enroute, 2Aug44, arrived and disembarked at Tinian, Marianas Islands and participated in the occupation and defence of Tinian, Marianas Islands.

THEO A. RYLANDER,
Capt, USMCR,
Commanding.

HEADQUARTERS
FIRST BASE HEADQUARTERS BATTALION
C/O FLEET POST OFFICE,
SAN FRANCISCO, CALIFORNIA

19 June 1945

The following is a transcript from original orders:

Embarked aboard the _____ at _____ and sailed therefrom on _____. Arrived at _____ and disembarked on _____.

RALPH E. GUINN,
Commanding.

Embarked aboard the USS JOSEPH T. DICKMAN at Peleliu on
21 July 45 and sailed therefrom on 22 July 45. Arrived and
disembarked at the Port of San Francisco, on 26 August 1945.

FRANK E. SESSIONS,
Major, USMC, Ret'd.

Corporal Allen J. Tillery's U.S. Marine Corps Professional Conduct Record

Corporal Allen J. Tillery, U.S.M.C. (center, without hat) and his
buddy, Private Fred N. Osgood, U.S.M.C., Tinian, 1944

Corporal Allen J. Tillery (center in t-shirt, cap askew) translating interrogation of recently captured Japanese soldiers for his Lieutenant (right in helmet), Marupo Wells, Tinian, 1944

Private Allen J. Tillery, U.S.M.C., Shreveport,
Louisiana (Rembrandt Studios), 1943

CHAPTER 5

Operation Forager
The Marianas

———

"Dimples eighty-two from North Tinian tower.
Take off to East on runway A for Able."

Tower to Colonel Paul Tibbets at
controls of <u>Enola Gay</u>, 2:45, a.m., August
6, 1945, North Field, Tinian Island

First Base Headquarters Battalion was being newly formed and was housed in several rows of tents in a far corner of the Center. Upon arrival I reported as directed and was assigned to a tent and told that I was attached to the battalion Intelligence Section under Colonel Clyde Metcalf.

I immediately liked the looks of this outfit. This was not the 22nd Marines. The troops were cleaner, better dressed and more G.I. The Marines that passed me in the company street were bright-eyed, happy and alert, unlike the sad, dull-eyed faces of the troops that I had left aboard ship in the lagoon at Eniwetok. This outfit was not trained to kill on a full-time basis. They had other seemingly more pleasant duties. I was certain that my chances for living a long and healthy life were greater here than on Guadalcanal. I was elated.

It was not long before I began to meet men whom I had known in the states. Bob Kraft and a man William Martin, both graduates of the Camp

Elliot Japanese Language School were in the Intelligence Section. I moved into a tent with them. It became apparent that the unit was being formed for the purpose of governing and controlling an island once organized resistance had ended. We would be the "Island Command" to take over when the assault troops were finished. The next objects of the forces being gathered by Admiral Nimitz would be larger islands with large civilian populations. Some sort of government or unified command of the island would be necessary after the fighting ceased. We would become that authority. This was a Headquarters Unit composed mostly of technically trained people, engineers, translators and interpreters, cartographers, medical teams and the usual array of clerks and office personnel.

We soon began training. A large amphibious operation was being planned against Japanese installations beyond the Marshalls. We were to be prepared to occupy and govern an island after it was pacified. We planned and trained for about one month. During this time, I was given liberty and on several occasions went into Honolulu and out to Waikiki. My mail finally caught up with me and at one mail call I received sixty letters. We were beginning to settle into a routine much like duty in the states.

On June 1 the routine was ended. We were confined to camp and were allowed to write no letters nor make any more telephone calls. We knew that we would be shipping out soon. Tommy Atkins' "troop-ship was on the tide."

Several days later we were placed aboard trucks and transported to the Naval Base at Pearl Harbor where we boarded the U.S.S. Sea Corporal. This was a typical troop-ship, however it was manned by merchant marine civilian sailors. Holds were full of bunks of canvas stretched between iron poles. The bunks were six high, one above the other. There were no ladders. Those who slept on high bunks merely climbed over the lower occupants to reach their beds. The holds were ill ventilated, hot, humid and constantly smelled of sweaty bodies, oil, saddle-soap and cigarettes.

Two days later, we departed Pearl Harbor down past Ford Island and Hickam Field out into the Pacific. We headed west. I had made this trip once before and I was apprehensive about this one. Again we joined a convoy. Soon the sea was covered with ships as far as one could see. Occasionally we saw carriers and battleships in the distance. Destroyers daily crossed near us on anti-submarine patrol.

Time moved slowly on board ship. We had no duties to perform. Kraft, Martin and I studied Japanese together on deck under the lifeboats. We translated some of the documents that I had captured at Eniwetok. Martin was our resident intellectual. He had been a college professor or at least a graduate student instructor prior to the war. He was equally adept at discussing Japanese or the history of Medieval Europe. Kraft had a great interest in the humanities as I did. We three spent many splendid evenings looking out over the Pacific and ruminating over the whole spectrum of the history of man. These were pleasant hours. We talked of our families, of the girls we left behind and of our hopes and plans for the future. These friendships were not soon forgotten. Both of these Marines were better educated than I was. I learned from them. My interests in literature and in history were expanded and reinforced by these discussions held on board this ship making its way across the Pacific. Both of these men touched my life. The imprint remains. Kraft would in later years become a medical doctor in California. In three months, Martin would be severely wounded by a Japanese grenade on Tinian and I would help to move him down a rocky hillside to a jeep to be transported to an aid-station. I never saw him again. I hope that he survived. He had much to live for.

Four days out of Hawaii, we were told that our destination was the Marianas Islands. The Task Force would assault and occupy Saipan, Tinian and Guam. Our unit would assume control of Tinian Island after the assault troops departed. We would mop up, restore order and prepare the Island for Seabees and engineers who would rebuild and expand the Japanese airfield already on the island to accommodate incoming B-29 Bombers. (Fourteen months later the <u>Enola Gay</u> would depart from one of these fields on Tinian and would drop the first atomic bomb on Hiroshima). We were given lectures on the history of Tinian, its physical makeup and the kind of civilian population that we would find there. Literature explaining all of this was given to the troops for further study.

We were aboard ship on June 6th when the ship's speaker announced that Allied Troops had landed on the beaches of Normandy opening the

Second Front. General Eisenhower's War was so far away that I do not believe that the news was of much importance to us. We had our own war to worry about.

The U.S.S. Sea Corporal arrived off Saipan on or about July 20th. Saipan, Tinian and Guam were the largest islands in the Marianas. Saipan and Tinian were only a few miles apart being separated by a narrow channel about three miles wide. The attack on Saipan had commenced on June 15th and the island was secure by the time of our arrival. The Fourth Marine Division assisted by the Second Marine Division in support began the assault on Tinian on July 24th, four days after our arrival in the area. We watched the bombardment of the beaches by the Navy and stood by as carrier planes bombed the island. For the first time in the Pacific War, napalm bombs were dropped on the Japanese. Napalm is a powder that produces a highly incendiary jelly when mixed with aircraft gasoline. We watched as these bombs scattered burning jelly over the targets. We later saw evidence of the effectiveness of this bomb when we went ashore.

On the evening of July 29th we were told that we would move onto Tinian Island the next morning. At 8:00 o'clock, July 30th, we were told to go over the side. We boarded large landing craft which were probably LCTs (landing craft tank) and headed for the beach. This was a much quieter landing than the previous three in which I had been involved. Our landing beaches were secure. We would not be met by hostile fire.

Tinian was about twelve miles long and about four miles across at its widest part. It was a pleasant island with an agricultural economy. It was laid out in neat patterns of fields and pastures marked by rows of trees. The land was fertile. There were wet and dry seasons that produced an abundance of rain and sunshine for crops. The principal crop was sugarcane. The island was covered with cane fields. Farmers lived about the island in small well-kept houses clustered in twos and threes. A fairly good system of roads covered the island. There was only one town on the island. Tinian Town was located in the south on Suharon Bay. A large sugar refinery was located near the town. The town had a few paved streets, masonry buildings and other less imposing structures where the populace lived. It must have been a nice quiet little town before we arrived. Papaya trees, mango and banana trees seemed to grow everywhere. The houses were covered with tropical vines and flowers.

Our landing craft dropped us off on a small beach in front of Tinian Town. The area was secure. The assault troops were still fighting about two miles to the south along the plateau that covered the end of the island. We could hear the sound of machine gun fire as well as the sound of artillery. The town was destroyed. Hardly a building was left standing. The sugar mill had been heavily damaged and vast quantities of syrup or molten sugar had flooded the area of the refinery as a result of the bombing. The sweet smell was nauseous. Clouds of flies and insects swarmed over the area. This smell combined with that of many unburied corpses was our welcome to Tinian Island.

We formed up, sent out scouts and began to move into the interior of the island. The area through which we moved had been the scene of a major battle only two days before. The refuse of combat was everywhere. Discarded weapons, ammunition boxes, burned out tanks and vehicles and dead Japanese soldiers were scattered over the area. We had been ordered to be alert as the battle was not finished. Stretcher bearers would frequently pass us bringing wounded marines to aid-stations in the rear. Sometimes these bearers were transporting dead Marines. Such a sight had a sobering effect on our unit most of whom were seeing these things for the first time.

We established camp a few miles northeast of the town around a cluster of damaged houses. For about thirty days we lived in pup tents, ate "C" rations and furnished security for the battalion. We arrived on Tinian at the beginning of the rainy season. For weeks the rain fell in solid sheets. Our tents flooded, our equipment molded and our camp besieged by rats who invaded our tents in an effort to escape the rain. I was awakened one night by a flashlight beam aimed at a huge rat on the tent pole only a few feet from my head. My tent mate was aiming a huge forty-five automatic pistol at the rat and probably would have blown the rat, the tent and me into the Pacific had not I counselled against such drastic action.

On August 1 most of the assault troops were withdrawn from the island. The 8th Marine Regiment was left on the southern plateau to continue operating against the Japanese who were still in hiding in caves and in jungle areas. The 8th Marines remained on Tinian until late in September. On several occasions I was ordered to accompany their patrols into the jungle areas surrounding the plateau to interrogate civilians that they flushed out of the jungle. Invariably these patrols were fired on by enemy soldiers who were hiding in caves hidden in the sides of the steep walls of the plateau. We fought back and killed a number of the enemy on each patrol. I was back in the War.

The rationale of the attack and occupation of Tinian was to obtain possession of several airfields that the Japanese had constructed on the island. These fields were to be repaired and the runways lengthened to accompany B-29s. The Japanese homeland was now within reach of our long range bombers. When these planes were able to fly off Tinian, the end of the war might be not far off.

The island soon became one giant construction project. Thousands of Seabees converged on the airfields and began the work required to enlarge the facilities. Towns and camps of Quonset huts were built to accommodate troops. Dozens of ships lay off Tinian Town disgorging all of the material required for the airfield projects.

The Island Command moved to a more permanent camp a few miles up the road. We moved into pyramidal tents with wooden floors. We had a real mess hall that .served hot chow or a regular basis. After cooking and warming our own food for more than thirty days, even powered eggs and spam was appreciated. I missed eating bread and can remember how good was the first meal in the new mess hall that included fresh bread. Battalion headquarters even had an office with typewriters and telephones connected to other installations on the island. With the telephone came civilization.

The eight thousand civilians who had survived the battle were relocated at Camp Churo on the northern end of the island. The camp was more like a town and was under the control of civil affairs officers who were subject to the Island Command. The intelligence Section of Island Command operated as a liaison between the camp and Battalion headquarters. We attempted to see that no enemy soldiers got into the camp masquerading as civilians. We also established contact with the Japanese civilian leaders for intelligence purposes.

It was the function of the Battalion intelligence Section to supply to the Island Commander such information as may affect the security of the island and the troops stationed there. From this somewhat nebulous duty there developed an operation that was to consume my energies for the next seven or eight months. It proved to be an exciting, humanly satisfying and constantly dangerous occupation.

Roads were being built to remote sections of the island to provide access to radar stations, anti-aircraft batteries and recreation facilities. Troops were beginning to move in every direction in pursuit of their duties. We began to get calls from outlying units advising us that they were being fired on as they worked. One day a Seabee was shot and killed while driving a truck along a quiet road. Guards on night duty at mess halls and warehouses killed several enemy soldiers who were trying to steal food and supplies. Our troops were being harassed and endangered by some of the hundreds of Japanese soldiers and civilians who had been hiding in caves and in the jungle areas along the southern plateau. They had simply melted into the jungles in front of the advancing assault troops and now lack of food and supplies was forcing them into the open. Many of these soldiers were armed and were still determined to fight. We also learned from civilian Japanese that many civilians including women and children were being prevented by the enemy soldiers from surrendering. We were not anxious to use flamethrowers and automatic weapons against women and children.

An order came down from the Island Commander — "muster up a posse and secure the area; destroy the soldiers and bring in the civilians."

Attached to the Battalion Intelligence Section was a scout patrol consisting of several Marines trained and armed to act as scouts for snipers. It was determined that these scouts assisted by others in the section would be formed into the unit required to carry out the General's order. The interpreters, Kraft, Martin and myself were to join the group to deal with civilians and with prisoners and to furnish three additional rifles. At first we numbered about fifteen and were led by Lt. Dale Chamberlain (Boulder, Colorado) and Sgt. Henry Eavis (Philadelphia, Pennsylvania). Chamberlain was an inexperienced but brave and resourceful officer. He would later die under a hail of machine gun fire while leading these same troops. Eavis, a veteran of the Guadalcanal campaign, was on his second tour of duty in the Pacific. He survived the war and occasionally at Christmastime I receive a card from him.

We were given ammunition, grenades and some automatic weapons (BAR) and a second-hand truck for transportation. On or about August 15 we made our first house call. Trucks using a road along the base of the plateau near Marpi (Marupo) Springs were being fired on from caves in the face of the cliffs. We took off for the Springs.

The truck was left at the base of the cliff and Chamberlain led us up the rocky sides. The area had previously been the scene of action. From time to time we stumbled over a decayed body or kicked a skull down the path. The debris of battle was everywhere. Our point was finally fired on by two enemy soldiers who quickly retreated into a large cave in the hillside. The patrol surrounded the cave. This was our first experience. It seemed logical that we should just toss in four or five grenades and blow them all up. However, our scouts had heard Japanese voices in the cave and we were concerned about the safety of women and children.

Chamberlain told me to crawl up to the cave and tell the occupants that they were surrounded and invite them to come out with their hands up minus their weapons. I was not overjoyed at this order. I crawled on my stomach to a large boulder about eight or ten feet from the entrance of the cave. I could smell the odor of cooking coming from the interior and hear muffled sounds from within. I looked back and saw fourteen rifles pointed at the cave from the rocks to my rear. I thought that if they fired they would get me first.

I called out to the Japanese telling them that they were surrounded and that if they put down their weapons and walked out with their hands up that no harm would come to them. I told them that the battle was over and that to die now was useless. I no sooner conveyed this message, than the soldiers in the cave began yelling "banzai", "banzai". We heard grenade explosions from within the cave. One soldier tried to run out and was killed at the entrance. The patrol poured a volley of fire into the cave. Then all was quiet. We waited for what seemed an interminable time. Finally, one by one we moved in close. From the entrance we could see four or five bodies. The enemy soldiers had pulled the pins on hand grenades and held them to their stomachs. The grenade was an awful substitute for the traditional short sword used in the act of <u>Seppuku</u> by which the samurai warrior disembowels himself when he is dishonored.

These soldiers simply could not face the prospect of surrender. It was a bloody scene. I thought of the St. Valentine's Day massacre along the infamous wall on Chicago's East Side. This was our first experience with the suicide of Japanese soldiers. We would see it many more times before we finished. We found rifles, ammunition, and grenades. We destroyed the cave and all the supplies. No more trucks would be fired on from this position.

It was late afternoon and the light was fading. The trees and vines cast strange and ominous shadows over the cave and the dead soldiers that we had dragged from their sanctuary. Everyone was anxious to leave.

Without looking back, we picked up our weapons and started down the rocky trail. We left the dead in front of the cave for the tropical sun, the insects and the small animals to reduce them to the dust to which man returneth. In a week they would resemble withered watermelons baking in the summer sun of a dry field, in four weeks only the bones would remain. We never buried Japanese dead. In the Marshalls where there were many, the bodies were thrown into deep holes dug out by a bulldozer and covered over with layers of sand. I suspect that this was more a measure of hygiene than of humanity. I have never thought much of this before. But, it is true. We killed them and left them in the caves and along the jungle trails where they fell. I do not ever recall being concerned about burial or disposition of the bodies. Perhaps someone else was assigned this duty. The Corps was highly specialized.

This small battle involving fifteen Marines and six or seven Japanese soldiers was a precursor of many to follow. During the next six months we repeated this scene over a hundred times. We blew up caves, staged ambushes, drove skirmish lines through cane fields to flush out the enemy and set traps with food and supplies. We killed a number of enemy soldiers and persuaded hundreds of civilians to leave the jungle and seek refuge in our camps. The problem of separating civilians from the military and the treatment of each was a constant problem.

The Soldiers

There were about 9,000 Japanese soldiers on Tinian Island when the Marines came ashore. They were under the command of Colonel Kiyoshi Ogata, a veteran of the Kwantung Army. Many of them were first class soldiers. The 50th Infantry Regiment of about 4,000 men had been brought to Tinian from Manchuria the previous spring. It was one of Japan's finest regiments. Many of these soldiers were veterans of the war in China. The majority of these troops were killed in the battle for possession of the island. Many survived the attack and probably as many as five hundred to eight hundred were hiding in the caves and jungle areas around the island. These were skilled and resourceful soldiers. They were armed and dedicated to striking a blow for the Emperor before they died. They gave no thought to surrender. It was these elusive and fanatical soldiers that we sought.

Our patrol went out several times each week. If they fired at our installations we hunted them down. Often we would find caches of food and we waited in ambush and killed the troops who came to recover it. We developed an intelligence system within the Japanese civilian camps and gained information from civilians who had recently been hiding in the jungle. Once or twice we even knew the name of the soldier that we hunted and how he was armed.

Unlike the campaign at Eniwetok, this was war on an individual basis. It was like trappers and frontiersmen hunting Indians along the Allegheny Trail. It was Drums Along the Mohawk. It was a personal fight. We saw the targets at which we fired and when our aim was good we viewed the results. We knew those of the enemy that we killed. I still have some of their diaries, dog tags, photographs and military insignia.

Many times we destroyed enemy troops by the mass fire of the patrol. I finally killed — saw him fall after pulling the trigger. He was older than I was. He wore glasses. A small man with two grenades in his belt and a rifle in his hand. He was trying to kill me. He was a corporal in an infantry regiment. That is all I know. That is all that I wanted to know. That was a long time ago.

There were lighter moments. A large open-air theatre was built near our camp and several times each week movies were shown. Hundreds of Marines viewed these movies sitting on sandbags that were formed into rows as seats. We once captured a young Japanese sailor who was trying to steal food from our mess hall. We fed him, treated a minor wound and kept him for a few days before sending him off to a prison camp. He spoke English quite well and some of the men in our unit enjoyed talking to him. For two weeks before his capture, he had seen every movie shown at our theatre. He could remember the names, the plots and knew some of the actors by name. While hiding in the surrounding woods he was entertained by the USO. I have heard such stories as this elsewhere and I am sure that it happened in other camps.

Japanese soldiers were brave, resourceful, well trained and absolutely fearless. They were formidable adversaries in the field. They did not want to be captured. They committed suicide or invited death at our hands rather than submit to becoming prisoners of war. Sometimes they were taken as prisoners because of illness, wounds or circumstances which they could not control. After capture when they finally realized that we would not kill them or torture them, they became cooperative, attentive to command and absolutely no trouble to handle. They had failed the Emperor. They had disobeyed the Imperial Rescript. Almost every Japanese soldier carried a small black book which was a copy of the <u>Imperial Mandates and Rescripts.</u> This little book contained the code of the Japanese soldier or sailor. It contained such phrases as "Death is lighter than a feather, but duty has the weight of mountains" and "It is better to die an honorable death than to suffer by the enemy." These Japanese soldiers could never go home. They became non-persons, suspended in limbo. I never saw a prisoner attempt to escape. They had no place to go.

From August 1, 1944 until I left Tinian on March 5, 1945, we were constantly engaged in this type of action. I could relate a dozen or more tales of firefights in cane fields, of blasting enemy soldiers from caves and of destroying campsites in jungle areas. The format was always the same and results inevitable. The work was hazardous. Of fifteen or sixteen men who served in the patrol, two were killed in action and two were seriously wounded and evacuated to Pearl Harbor.

Lieutenant Chamberlain and Private First Class Lonnie Davis (Weatherford, Texas) were both killed by automatic weapons in a night ambush at

Marupo Springs. They were buried in crude wooden coffins beneath white crosses in the cemetery near the north end of the island where the Marines had first come ashore in the initial attack. I have often wondered if they were brought back to the huge military cemetery in the Punch Bowl at Honolulu.

Gunnery Sergeant Saul Marcus and Martin, the interpreter, were both wounded by a Japanese grenade thrown from a cave after Martin had moved in close to call for surrender. We thought that the cave housed civilians. It did not.

One observation is required at this point. This concerns my comments about and my memories of the Japanese soldier. When I arrived in the Central Pacific during the first days of January, 1944, it was obvious to all rational observers that an American victory was simply a matter of time. The armada that Admiral Spruance unleashed on the Marianas consisted of 800 ships plus perhaps 1,000 carrier based aircraft. A Japanese defeat was inevitable to all but the most fanatical samurai. I saw the Japanese soldier in defeat, in death or as a prisoner of war. He fought hard, died well, but became a model prisoner if captured.

I am not unmindful of the barbarous actions of some Japanese as arrogant victors in battle. The Bataan death march, atrocities committed against our airmen who were shot down during the Battle of Midway and many other recorded instances of cruelty toward prisoners are sufficient to forever mar the honor of the Japanese military. I saw none of this and as a result my personal observations of the Emperor's troops are simply different from those made at other times and other places.

When my brother, Jim, fought the Japanese at Guadalcanal with the Marine Raiders in August of 1942, an American victory was by no means certain. On at least one occasion, Japanese air supremacy forced Admiral Fletcher to withdraw the U.S. Fleet with its protective air umbrella from the combat zone leaving the Marines on the beaches and their unarmed transports to the mercy of the Imperial Navy. Had Yamamoto's fleet prevailed, the Marines would have been left to die in the jungles of the Solomon Islands. My brother's memories of the war differ from mine. He faced a Japanese army that had never known defeat and a fleet that was in many ways superior to that of Nimitz and Halsey. By the time the 22nd Marines stormed the beaches of Eniwetok in 1944, Jim and his comrades had beaten some of the arrogance out of the Japanese army. We latecomers reaped the benefit of their endeavors.

Tinian was ten miles long with a maximum width of five miles. Mount Lasso, its highest point, was 564 feet above the Pacific. The southern plateau near Marupo Point was a rugged, rocky area covered with dense foliage. The Patrol covered every foot of the island from Ushi Point in the North to Lalo Point at the southern tip. We went out on a mission several times each week. We searched caves, destroyed camp sites and killed Japanese soldiers on a weekly basis.

The Navy had provided us with a portable battery-operated loudspeaker that we carried with us into the jungle areas. When we cornered the enemy in a cave or in a dense area, Kraft, Martin, or I would use the device to attempt to induce the Japanese to surrender. We would tell them in Japanese that the battle was finished, that the Japanese Fleet had returned to the homeland (Naichi) and that to die was senseless. We assured them of good treatment. The civilians would surrender. The soldiers would not. Often the soldiers would prevent the civilians from surrendering. The civilians in hiding included women, children and often babies and elderly people. It is one thing lo kill a child or a young woman by the impersonal firing of a naval cannon from two or three miles off shore or the dropping of a bomb from 30,000 feet, but quite another to do so with a rifle or grenade from 25 feet. This posed a dilemma for the Marines in the Patrol. Survival required instant reaction to supposed danger. Humanity required patience and caution. Killing was easy. Discretion was moral but often dangerous.

THE CIVILIANS

Prior to the War, the native Chamorros had been moved from Tinian to other islands in the Marianas. The civilian population of some 15,000 Japanese were farmers or employees of the South Seas Development Corporation (Nan-Yo Kohatsu Kaisha) who worked in the sugar mill at Tinian Town. The Japanese civilian leaders were all part of the Southeast Asia Co-Prosperity Sphere, This was an imperial attempt to colonize the South Seas.

Most of the civilian population had surrendered to the Marines of the assault force prior to my arrival on the Island, They were interned at Camp Churo at the north end of Tinian. Civil affairs people from the Navy were establishing a civilian government and creating the kinds of services required to feed, house and govern a small town.

Several thousand civilians remained in hiding all over the island in caves and other isolated sanctuaries. Most of them were situated in the areas of the Southern Plateau which was a heavily wooded and rocky area of cliffs and ravines. Many soldiers had assumed civilian disguise and had infiltrated the encampments. They had weapons and were natural leaders in such an environment. Our task was to persuade them to surrender without further loss of life.

Our intelligence as to the location of these civilian groups came from several sources. Scouts located their water supplies, followed their trails from storage areas from which they stole supplies and tracked them down by sight and smell. Previously captured civilians, secure in the knowledge that the Americans provided humane treatment to prisoners, came to us with information about relatives and friends whose lives they wanted to save.

The Patrol would travel to areas in which we believed civilians were hiding, After securing the area, the interpreters would by loud speaker announce our presence to the Japanese and tell them to come out and join their friends and relatives at Camp Churo. I often assured them of safe treatment. I told them that the war for Tinian was over. Hundreds of civilians heeded our plea. Often as many as 30 or 40 men, women and children would come out of the caves or jungle hiding places with their hands up. They were astounded to be met by rugged looking Marines with automatic weapons offering them candy and cigarettes and kind words.

On some occasions, our plea for surrender would be met by gunfire or grenade blasts. Japanese soldiers would seldom surrender and were prepared to kill civilians who did. It was this activity that caused the death of Lieutenant Chamberlain, PFC Davis and the wounding of Sergeant Marcus and William Martin,

During eight months of operations, we persuaded in excess of 800 civilians to come out of hiding and return to friends and relatives at Camp Churo. We fed the starving, comforted the fearful, tended the wounded, clothed the naked and delivered two babies. We were aided by many intelligent and sensitive Japanese civilians who knew that living was preferable to dying. Hataya San, the Mayor of Churo and Toshio Yamashina, his deputy, were two brave and good men who did much to aid and relieve their stricken people. I worked closely with these two Japanese officials for many months. They were the first Japanese that I knew as human beings rather than faceless enemies. There would be more later.

Often we took Hataya or Yamashina with us on patrol so that they could call to the civilians in the caves and jungles and ask them to come in. They were most successful as they were calling to friends and fellow workers who trusted them to tell the truth. Sometime in December, Hataya told the Civil Affairs Director at Camp Churo that there were men in the camp who believed that their wives or children or relatives were being held in caves in the Carolinas (Karorinasu) Area and were being prevented from coming to safety by soldiers. These people were starving and were in danger of being killed by Marine search parties. The men wanted to be set free in the suspected area overnight or for several days so as to find their families and persuade them to surrender. This message was passed to Colonel Metcalf and it was agreed that such action be tried. On more than one occasion we took Japanese civilians onto the southern plateau and released them for several days. On each occasion they returned at the appointed time bringing in more civilians from the caves and hills.

In at least two instances we were asked by a Japanese civilian to give him a weapon so that he could persuade the Japanese soldiers to release his wife or father from the caves. We did this twice and probably became the first U.S. Marines to provide a Japanese prisoner with a pistol and set him free. Our trust was never violated.

Early one December morning, the 15 men of the unit journeyed to a small farm house on a flat plain over Marupo Springs to rendezvous with some Japanese civilians whom we had released a few days earlier. We located the trail from which the Japanese would appear, set up a tight defense perimeter and settled in to wait. About 9 o'clock, our man appeared on the trail and gave the password. He walked into the clearing amid the mango trees, approached me and from a large brown sack that he carried he carefully dumped a white skull and an array of bones at my feet. He pointed to the bones and said, "Kawamoto desu."

"How do you know that it is Kawamoto?" I asked.

He pulled a tarnished bronze medal from his pocket and handed it to me while he explained that his friend had won the medal at the Olympic games in Los Angeles in 1932 and always wore it on his belt. The Olympic winner had died in the battle for Tinian months before.

Everyone learned to speak a few words of Japanese. We employed civilian Japanese to work on roads and in our camps. It was necessary for their guards (Hancho) to be able to issue simple orders. Members of our patrol needed a few words to deal with Japanese military prisoners. The Language Section prepared a list of phrases in Japanese and English to be used by the Marines.

hands up	te wo agete
advance	susume
come out	de-te ko-i
halt	tomare
take your clothes off	fuku wo nuge

The last was particularly important. In all John Wayne movies, Japanese soldiers would feign surrender while concealing grenades in their clothes to be used on unsuspecting Marines. I never saw this occur and never knew anyone who did, but it was difficult to deny John Wayne and Metro-Goldwyn-Mayer. When enemy soldiers surrendered they were told "te wo agete, fuku wo nuge!" – "hands up, clothes off!" Members of our patrol became adept at yelling these phrases at prisoners as they came out of the jungle areas or the caves. Japanese prisoners in the Pacific were usually stripped to their fundoshi (G-string) at time of surrender.

In one of our last actions on Tinian, we discovered a large group of civilians hiding in a deep cave among the rocks at Lalo Point. We surrounded the area and used the speaker to assure them of safe conduct if they would come out. A white flag soon appeared at the entrance to the cave and an ancient Japanese woman carrying a small baby came out followed by about 15 other civilians. They were sent to the rear for safety.

We again tried to persuade the remaining persons to surrender. After several minutes, another flag appeared and a Japanese girl of about twenty walked toward us from the cave. She wore a white kimono type dress, obviously freshly washed, which emphasized her long black hair, slender figure and regal bearing. As if acting on command, the entire Marine detachment stood up, leveled their weapons at the girl and yelled, "fuku wo nuge!" Without a moment's hesitation, the girl looked at her captors with disdain, held her head high and walked right between two M-1 rifles to join her family in the rear.

Life on the island moved slowly during the fall and winter months of 1944. Living conditions improved as more facilities were constructed. We lived in pyramidal tents with crushed coral floors and slept on regulation army cots. The food was fair if not fresh. Powdered milk, powdered eggs, dehydrated vegetables and canned meats were served in the mess hall. We saw movies a few times each week and occasionally a live U.S.O. show with real girls. Mail from the States was received regularly. This was the greatest morale builder of all. Beer arrived on Tinian in November. Each man received a ration of two bottles per week served warm.

The old Japanese airfield at Ushi Point was repaired and new runways were constructed to accommodate the B-29 bombers of the 21st Bombardment Group. In late November over 100 B-29s flew out of Tinian's North Field on a 1,500 mile trip to stage the first mass raid on Tokyo. We knew little of these activities. We saw the huge bombers leave and return. We suspected their destination. The War was being delivered to the Japanese homeland from whence it came by super-fortresses flying from our island. The strategic significance of all of this was wasted on a twenty year old Marine. I just wanted to go home.

Christmas came and provided us with a turkey dinner and midnight services in the chapel which were interrupted by a Japanese air raid. Occasionally a lone Japanese plane would fly down from Rota or one of the other Japanese islands in the Marianas that had been bypassed and attempt to bomb the airfields on Tinian. I do not believe that they ever did drop a bomb. However our antiaircraft fire and searchlights provided a spectacular display of pyrotechnics for our Christmas enjoyment.

In one week I would begin my second year overseas. Marines were not usually returned to the States until after two years of foreign duty. I had a long way to go. Most of us at this time did not see any immediate end to the War in the Pacific. Conversations always included thoughts about fighting in China, Manchuria and about assault landings on Honshu or Kyushu. Our experience did not indicate to us that the Japanese would surrender until they were totally destroyed. Most of us were looking forward to a long, long war.

In early February, 1945, I arrived at our Section Headquarters one morning to relieve the guard at 6 o'clock A.M. After pouring a cup of coffee and reading the log for the night, I walked into the Colonel's office and saw a stack of four or five bound volumes on a table which had not been there the previous day. Each volume was several inches thick and stamped on the cover of each were the words "Top Secret" in large letters. The documents were designated as the complete operation's plans for the assault and capture of Iwo Jima. I had never seen anything like it before. I examined the plans which designated the units, ships and times of attack as well as logistical support. It was a strange place for such sensitive documents to be carelessly deposited. When the Colonel came in they disappeared and I never saw them again.

A few days later the Iwo Jima task force began to assemble in the anchorage between Saipan and Tinian. Soon hundreds of ships including transports, battleships, cruisers and carriers were standing off the islands. Lieutenant Chamberlain had never been quite satisfied with the limited action on Tinian and had long desired to participate in a major amphibious operation. During the months that we had served on Tinian, he made several attempts to have the entire patrol transferred to some unit of the Iwo Jima task force that was then being assembled. He even made a trip to Saipan to see if such a transfer could be arranged. The members of the patrol did not favor his efforts. We were perfectly happy with our own little war. We did not require escalation.

One morning we awoke to discover that the entire armada had disappeared. A few weeks later when we began to receive the reports of the bloody action on the beaches of Iwo Jima, we were thankful that the Lieutenant had failed.

A few weeks after his return from Saipan, Lieutenant Chamberlain was dead. There was enough war for everyone. For Mr. Roberts. For Lieutenant Chamberlain. One need only bide his time.

Marine Lieutenant Walter Harrison (Seattle, Washington) replaced the dead Chamberlain as the Patrol Commander and led the unit in its final two months of operations. Harrison came to us with no combat experience. He proved himself an able young officer in the finest tradition of the Corps. Like Chamberlain, he was not afraid to lead. The Marine officers with whom I fought possessed this virtue. They were in the forefront of every attack. They were highly visible in battle. The percentage of casualties among Marine platoon commanders was frightfully high.

The new year brought a change of command on the island. By the first days of January, 1945, civilization had taken hold of Tinian and was remaking it in the image of Long Beach. Traffic cops were directing traffic at busy intersections, every office possessed a telephone or two, the PX was selling Hershey Bars, Baby Ruths and Lucky Strikes. The biggest business on the island was created by the horde of sailors coming ashore from ships parked in the anchorage to look at a real battlefield. They were suckers for souvenirs. Some of the Marines found a supply of Japanese parachutes. When these were cut into small squares and decorated with the rising sun painted in the middle surrounded by a few Japanese characters (Kanji), they became valued samurai battle flags. A little red paint to simulate blood made them more valuable. For a small percentage of the action, Kraft and I painted Japanese characters on a lot of flags. I am sure that even now there are probably a few homes in these United States where occasionally some ex-sailor proudly shows a samurai flag to his grandchildren that bears the words in Japanese "United States Marine Corps" – which were the characters that I do best.

The collection of souvenirs and other mementos of battle was an activity to which much time was devoted. Most of the troops would cheerfully risk their lives, and often did, to acquire a samurai sword or a Japanese battle flag. The flags we could manufacture. The swords had to be taken from their owners. The quality of the souvenir depended upon the time of acquisition. The assault forces that did the fighting were first on the scene. They scooped up everything of value – swords – flags – officers' pistols – watches –Suntory whiskey and personal items taken from enemy dead. The occupation troops such as Island Command came a bit later and took those things which were passed over by the combat regiments - some good - some not so good. The Seabees, engineer units, air force and naval land forces came much later and were required to purchase souvenir items. A samurai sword could bring five hundred dollars in the ward room of a carrier or battleship.

The Intelligence Section of Island Command was authorized by Jicpoa (Joint Intelligence Corps Pacific Ocean Area) to pass judgment on souvenirs and mementos being sent out in the U.S. Mail. All such items being mailed to the States required a Jicpoa stamp of approval. The language staff at Battalion Headquarters was given this responsibility. We examined every question-able item before it was mailed. The troops sent some strange items –Japanese shoes – furniture – eyeglasses – spent bullets – shell casings – diaries – letters and books written in Japanese and teeth (which were rejected).

Seabees were the most ingenious of the souvenir senders. A carpenters-mate arrived one day with an ashtray made from a Japanese skull. He found the skull on some contested field, cleaned end polished it and applied a clear lacquer finish. He cut a round hole in the top of the skull and placed therein the large end of a brass 40 millimeter shell casing which had been cut down to about three inches and highly polished. The skull was placed upon and attached to a polished wooden base. A small metal sign under the grinning skull proclaimed "Remember Pearl Harbor." It was an objet d'art. Colonel Metcalf confiscated the ashtray and the Seabee barely escaped the firing squad. As a result of the investigation prompted by this bit of art, an order went out from the Island Commander requiring all Seabee truck drivers to remove the Japanese skulls which they displayed as radiator ornaments on their trucks while driving about the island.

Marines do not do well in civilization. Like certain ferns and rhododendrons, they thrive in the boondocks. It was time to move on. In early January, Army Brigadier General Frederick V.H. Kimble replaced Marine General James Underhill as the Island Commander. Army troops began moving in and the word was passed that First Base Headquarters Battalion would be disbanded and its troops transferred to other Marine units. Piece by piece, we were taken apart. Army Captain Sam Weintraub (New York) came in to replace Lieutenant Harrison and operated with us for a few months. He was a good and dependable officer. Army Major Charles Erb was sent in to replace Colonel Metcalf who went home to rest and retire. At an age surely in excess of sixty, he never should have been there in the first place. Old Charlie Erb was a simple minded soul who had been a football hero at the University of California in 1924. He was a danger to the Japanese, to the Marines and to himself. A merciful God decreed that we served under him for only a short time. He went on one mission with us. When we got out of his jeep in the jungle to follow a trail, he took his pistol out of the holster, handed it to me and said, "Son, load this thing for me and show me how to put the safety off," I just knew that my day for the Purple Heart had finally arrived.

On March 4 our orders arrived. The Intelligence Section of Island Command was relieved of duty on Tinian and re-assigned to the Island Command on Guam. This was good news. Kraft and I were to be assigned to the Japanese Prisoner of War Camp on Guam. Instead of killing and capturing Japanese soldiers, we would be dealing with those already disarmed and subdued. A few days later, we said goodbye to those friends who remained on Tinian, boarded an LST and departed for Guam a few hundred miles to the South.

I had spent eight months on Tinian. There I had seen my first Christmas overseas and had celebrated my twentieth birthday. The amphibious war in the Marshalls was battle in all its classic fury – exploding shells, dive-bombers, machine guns, flamethrowers, assault charges and dead and dying in multiple figures. On Tinian, I had seen another side of the war a personal side – a quiet side – killing in multiples of one. I had been a witness to war visited on a large civilian population - dead women and children, frightened and hungry babies, displaced families and destroyed homes. All of this, together with dead Marines who had died six thousand miles from home on an island whose name they had not known until three months before they died.

In the early hours before dawn August 6, 1945, six months after we departed from Tinian, the <u>Enola Gay</u> piloted by Colonel Paul Tibbets roared down the extended runway of the old Japanese airfield at Ushi Point carrying the atomic bomb to Hiroshima on a trip which, like that of Columbus four centuries before, would change the course of history for untold generations.

I would not forget Tinian. No one who ever saw a photograph of the mushroom cloud over Hiroshima would ever forget Tinian.

CHAPTER 6

Guam

———

"A POW is required to give only his name, rank and service number."

GENEVA CONVENTIONS OF 1929

THE VOYAGE TO GUAM TOOK only one day. Enroute we passed Rota, one of the enemy held islands that had been by-passed by Admiral Nimitz and left to die of neglect. Its airfield was demolished and its defenders isolated from any help from Tokyo. It was strange to pass so close to an island still occupied by Japanese troops armed and ready for battle. They were rendered useless without the cost of one American Marine.

Magellan, who claimed it for Spain in 1521, called it Isla de Los Ladrones (Island of Thieves); the United States, who acquired it in 1898 after the Spanish-American War, called it Guam; the Japanese who captured it on December 12, 1941 called it <u>Omiya Jima</u> (Great Shrine Island). When I arrived there in early March 1945, the Island was again called Guam by courtesy of the United States Marines.

By any name, Guam is an imposing island. It is 25 miles long and about 6 or 7 miles wide. Mount Lamlam, its highest point, towers 1300 feet over a verdant jungle. Other mountains and uplands were interspersed between plateaus covered with kunai grass and heavy jungle growth. It was a rugged place.

The battle for Guam had ended on August 10th of the previous year when Marine General Roy Geiger announced that organized resistance had ceased. Early in 1945, Admiral Nimitz brought his flag to Guam and established CinCPAC Headquarters in new buildings erected on the Fonte Plateau. The Commander-in-Chief wanted to be close to Iwo Jima and Okinawa to which his attention would be soon given. Like Tinian, Guam had become a giant staging area from which future operations against the Empire of Hirohito would be provisioned. General Curtis LeMay had established his headquarters of the 21st Bombardment Group on the island. This headquarters was directing B-29 Superfortresses in firebombing raids that were daily reducing Japan's major cities to heaps of rubble. The command decisions that would set in motion forces that would destroy the Japanese Empire were then being formulated in headquarters' buildings scattered about the island.

Upon arrival at Apra Harbor, we were loaded into a 6 x 6 truck driven up a mountain and deposited at the Prisoner of War Camp, The compound was a typical Hollywood type POW Camp. It was about 350 yards long and about 150 yards wide completely surrounded by two very high barbed wire fences about six feet apart. Guard dogs patrolled the perimeter inside these fences. Towers were erected at each corner of the enclosure that were manned by guards armed with machine guns. Other armed guards patrolled the area and operated the gate.

There were about 300 prisoners in the camp when I arrived. I had never seen so many living Japanese soldiers. The prisoners were housed in native style huts with thatched roofs. They slept on the ground on woven mats called tatamis. The prisoners cooked and served their own meals and in general ran the camp. The area was clean, orderly and well managed. The POWs left the compound daily on work details to which they were assigned about the island. They were housed well and fed well. I never saw a prisoner mistreated. They had plenty of leisure time during which they played baseball or volleyball. The more gentle souls played chess (shogi) and a similar game called go.

The presence of the interpreters and language personnel was necessary to an orderly administration of the camp. For this reason we were assigned living quarters adjacent to the compound. We lived in a native hut with a thatched roof and a crushed coral floor. We slept on army cots and unlike Tinian mosquito nets were required for sound sleeping. The living conditions on Guam were excellent. For the first time in eight months, I did not run the risk of being shot during each day's work. The food was good, movies frequent and a well-stocked PX available.

We were assigned to work with two Navy Lieutenants who were graduates of the Navy Japanese Language School at Boulder, Colorado. This school commissioned its graduates after a year of study. Both of these men were acutely aware of the gap between officers and enlisted men and were constantly on guard to preserve this distance. I spoke Japanese better than either of them and often enjoyed the advantage. Cal Dunbar (Los Angeles), a graduate of the Language School at Camp Elliott, was also attached to the POW camp. It was a pleasure to meet him again. He presently lives in West Yellowstone, Montana, and we occasionally correspond in somewhat rusty Japanese. The two officers, Kraft, Dunbar and I handled the work of translating and interpreting in all areas of camp management.

In addition to this pedestrian chore, we also interrogated prisoners and wrote reports for Navy Intelligence based on these conversations.

At the time of my arrival at the camp, most of the prisoners held there had been captured on Guam or on Iwo Jima. A few isolated ones were brought in by submarine or were Japanese pilots who had been shot down near American installations. The ones from Iwo were important. They were newly captured and many had been in Japan only a few months before their capture. They possessed important information. Each interpreter was assigned a number of prisoners for interrogation. We had a format to follow and certain designated questions to ask. The answers that we elicited were incorporated into our reports. These reports together with our comments from expanded conversations were forwarded to Pearl Harbor for further study by Jicpoa. We never knew how the information was used. We never knew what was really important. We asked the questions and recorded the answers. At 20 years old and with a limited knowledge of Japanese my contribution to naval intelligence was limited.

Japanese prisoners were in general cooperative, friendly, talkative and a source of much information. A Japanese soldier or sailor was taught from the date of his enlistment never to surrender and never to submit to capture. He was told to fight and to die if necessary. The Emperor preferred his death to his surrender. His spirit could never rest at the hallowed Shrine of Yasukuni if he surrendered. He believed this without reservation. One needed to understand this attitude to fully appreciate the kami-kaze mentality of the Japanese military. It would have been an anomaly to teach a soldier never to surrender or submit to capture – but, just in the unlikely event that you do this dishonorable act, then give only your name, rank and service number. It always appeared to us that not much had been said to the Japanese soldiers about what to do if captured. Of the many enemy soldiers that I interviewed, only one ever mentioned the Geneva Convention. They would of course avoid answering pointed questions for very obvious reasons. However, rarely ever would they refuse to answer general questions or deny having information that we knew they possessed.

Our days were busy but our duties were not structured. We performed at our own pace. The weather was mild, the surroundings pleasant and the work intellectually stimulating. We were not required to participate in any military formations nor was any particular dress required of us. We usually slept late in the mornings and thus avoided breakfast in the mess hall. We ate breakfast with the Japanese cooks in the compound. As I walked about the camp, the prisoners bowed good-morning, "Tirere San, Ohayo Goziamas." Sometimes they called me Gocho San (corporal). We were treated with great deference.

We spent many hours talking to the prisoners. They never talked of going home. This was not to be. They talked of America or of Brazil or Argentina. My language ability improved with practice. I picked up the idiom and increased my vocabulary. Many times I was asked how long I had lived in Japan. I had memorized an address in Tokyo from some bit of correspondence that I had picked up on Tinian. When asked this question, I used to throw out the address. One day a prisoner told me that his uncle lived in a district near that address. We translated the camp commander's orders into

Japanese, settled disputes between prisoners and attended sick call and interpreted between physician and patient.

BASEBALL

The Japanese have always been avid baseball fans. Many of them were well acquainted with the names of America's famous baseball players. They played ball almost every evening after work. One day a group of prisoners arrived from Iwo. They were dirty, ragged and frightened as were all POWs when first admitted to the camp. As they walked down the main street one tall POW seemed to be attracting a great deal of attention. The prisoners were bowing to him and talking about him. I asked a young Jap sailor who spoke some English about this newcomer. He said, "He Japanese Basu-Baru; he Japanese Babu-Ruthu."

Later when the famous ball player became accustomed to captivity, he would pinch-hit at ball games. He always had a runner. I never saw him do anything but hit. Of course, he was a major.

CANNIBALISM

When I first arrived at the POW camp, I had noticed two prisoners who were kept in a hut isolated from the others. They both had distended stomachs as is sometimes seen on people who are starving or suffering from malnutrition. I was told that while they were hiding in the jungle from the Marines that they had cooked and eaten a young Japanese soldier in order to appease their hunger. I did not know whether they had killed the soldier or whether he had been consumed after a natural death.

One day I was told to accompany two officers, a doctor and some military police who were to gather evidence of this deed. We checked two prisoners out of the stockade, boarded a truck and headed into the jungle. After about an hour's ride and a long walk along a sandy beach, the Japs showed us the remains of a camp where they had hidden during the battle and for several months thereafter. We found the remains of a campfire, iron cooking pots and a collection of large bones from which the meat had been cooked or cut.

The doctor seemed to indicate that these were human bones. All of this was collected by the military police, tagged and placed in bags for delivery back to the stockade headquarters.

A few days later, the two prisoners were taken away. We heard that they were to be tried for the offense by a military tribunal. Just what law would form the basis of a charge against them was somewhat obscure.

Unusual problems require unusual solutions. So it was said at Nuremberg and elsewhere.

CRIME AND PUNISHMENT

A small valley separated the POW stockade from the marine brig. The brig was constructed like the POW camp only on a smaller scale. There was incarcerated in this brig Marine and Naval personnel who had been convicted of theft, assault and battery, rape, attempted murder and other violations of naval law (rocks and shoals). The Jap POWs and Naval prisoners viewed each other across the small crevasse.

The inhumane treatment of prisoners in a marine brig was probably only exceeded by that of Auschwitz or Dachau. Marine Corps recruiters had a talent for selecting a number of mean, sadistic bastards. These individuals were immediately assigned to guard duty at naval prisons and marine brigs. Shortly after the War, several formal investigations revealed a pattern of ill and sadistic treatment of prisoners in Marine Corps brigs.

Some of the methods of handling marine prisoners by their guards almost defied belief. When prisoners were first admitted to a brig, their hair was cut down to the scalp and they were given green dungarees with a large "P" printed on both front and back of the jacket. Prisoners never walked. They always moved at double-time. When they halted, they immediately folded their arms over their chest. Many of them marched with leg irons and some shackled with a ball and chain. They were constantly followed by heavily armed guards who berated them for every minor infraction of rules. They worked from dawn until dusk. How they ate and slept I do not know.

I saw this conduct both at Camp Elliott in California and also on Guam. I believe that it was standard practice in the Corps. Some of the treatment was probably justified. I do know that there were men in these brigs for minor infractions of military justice who did not deserve nor require such extreme punishment. 1945 was a long way from Tun's Tavern.

One of the recreation areas of the POW camp was directly across from the marine brig. Often in the late evening I would go there to talk to the prisoners. They expressed sympathy for the marine prisoners across the way. More than one Jap told me that he much preferred being a prisoner of war.

ONE LAST CHANCE FOR A PURPLE HEART

Guam was a very large island heavily wooded with few populated areas. Seven months after the fighting had ended many armed Japanese soldiers were still hiding in the jungles. They were perfectly willing to fight one more battle for the Emperor. I do not know if there was any organized attempt to secure their capture or demise as there had been on Tinian. Occasionally a POW would be taken out by the military police who were to be led to locations at which enemy soldiers were presumed to be hiding. In this fashion, I was destined to make one final patrol.

Shortly after Easter, the younger of our two lieutenants told me to meet him at the stockade gate at dawn the next day for a trip into the jungle. I was instructed to bring a weapon and live ammunition. Apparently I was going back to war. My carbine required cleaning. I had not needed it since leaving Tinian.

I reported as ordered in field uniform, canteen, steel helmet and carbine with several clips of ammunition. The lieutenant showed up in neat khaki accompanied by two Japanese soldiers who had come in from the boondocks a few weeks before. His only concession to the occasion was a sidearm.

I was told that our guides were to show us a camp in the bush where two enemy soldiers were living. They would surrender when we arrived. Our lack of firepower indicated to me that the place must be close by. I was directed to a back seat in the jeep with one Jap while the other joined the officer in the front. We took off down the main road to Agana.

We passed through the town and soon left the main road for a smaller path near the beach. I became apprehensive as we drove deeper and deeper into the jungle. We seemed to be alone and far away from any civilization. We had been driving for more than an hour when the lieutenant pulled off the road onto a caribou trail and after a few minutes driving stopped in the front yard of a deserted native house. We seemed to be miles from any military establishment. Several times I had cautioned the officer as to the dangerous position that we were in. He ignored me and indicated that he knew just what he was doing. I began to doubt this. I loaded my carbine and observed the jungle around us very carefully.

I was told to stay at the house with one of the soldiers while the lieutenant joined the other Jap for a hike of about 2 miles down the beach to the sanctuary. By this time I was frantic. I knew that this naval officer was totally out of his element and had placed both of us in an extremely precarious situation. Armed enemy soldiers were constantly on the move in the jungle, I protested to no avail. This was 1945 and corporals obeyed lieutenants. He took off into the bush with one Jap leaving me with the other to await his return.

The jungle around us was so thick that visibility was limited to about fifty feet. We were surrounded by hundreds of palm trees, many of which soared a hundred feet into the air above the jungle. Very little light filtered through the foliage and we were almost in semi-darkness. I just knew that I would not get out of that place alive. The house had no walls and was completely open. I thought it best to get away from the open area. The Jap and I cleared a small area in a corner of the yard and settled in to wait.

I remembered the terrible night on Eniwetok. That first night of crouching in a foxhole while Japs screamed and flares drifted over the island to reveal the awful carnage of battle. I was once again frightened and also angry at myself for allowing an inexperienced nut to put me in this position.

We waited. I jumped at every sound – birds – falling coconuts – parrots – land crabs and caribou. The POW and I talked in whispers. He was certain that I would shoot him if anyone attacked us and he was probably right. I wondered about an ambush. A trap. We waited for five hours. I never relaxed a muscle.

The sun passed overhead, the shadows changed and afternoon was upon us. I began to wonder about the night. Surely, not all night. Then it happened. The lieutenant burst out of the jungle. He left with one Jap and returned with one Jap. Those that he sought had fled. Let's go home!

We started for the jeep. Could it be possible that the enemy troops were following us? I kept waiting to hear a bolt snap shut – the crack of an Arisaka rifle – the whine of a .31 caliber bullet. I brought up the rear glancing over my shoulder all the way.

We boarded the jeep and went home. It was a dumb thing to have done. We were fortunate that we did not meet enemy soldiers. They were there.

In 1965, just twenty years after the lieutenant and I left that jungle clearing, the Associated Press reported that three Japanese soldiers surrendered to a policeman on Guam.

BANZAI REQUIEM

Most of the Japanese that I had encountered prior to arrival at Guam, both civilian and military, were of peasant heritage. They were small farmers, factory workers, clerks and trades people. Most were lower school graduates (sho-gakko). This was equivalent to an elementary education in the United States. They were literate, understood math and some physical science. They had a very limited education in the areas of economics, geography and world history. They had no depth of understanding of the causes of the War or what the results might be for the Empire if they were defeated. They simply assumed that they would die and spend eternity in spirit form at Yasukuni.

At the POW camp I began to meet a different kind of prisoner. I met officers for the first time. There was a vast gap between officers and enlisted men in the Japanese army. More so than in our own. The Samurai tradition of the officer corps was strong. A number of officers had been captured at Iwo. I met a graduate of the Imperial University of Tokyo (Tokyo Dai-Gakko).

These POWs were sometimes handled by officers from CinCPAC who were fluent in Japanese and conversant with international politics as well as future war plans.

One day while doing a routine interrogation of a newly arrived prisoner, I discovered that only six months previous to his capture, he had been employed in the Japanese Foreign Ministry in Tokyo in some minor capacity. At one time he had worked for Prince Konoye. He wanted to discuss the War, how it began and how it could best be ended quickly. He was an intellectual of sorts, well educated and quite ready to discuss sensitive areas of military intelligence. My expertise was soon exhausted. After my report was filed, he was spirited away into the bowels of CinCPAC Intelligence. He probably never saw another corporal.

By the end of March Iwo Jima was secured. Fighter planes based there could protect the B-29s all the way to Tokyo. Tojo's air power was non-existent. Our command of the air over Japan was virtually complete. The super-forts were beginning to annihilate the major cities of Honshu. Vast areas of Tokyo were devastated by fire-bombs. The landings on Okinawa were commenced on April 1 and the island was secure on May 31. The fleets of Admirals Spruance and Halsey ranged over the Western Pacific without opposition. The great ships of the once vaunted Combined Fleet of Isoroku Yamamoto lay buried in graves all over the Pacific from Midway to Leyte Gulf. The War was won. Only the fanaticism of the Japanese military kept it going. With this in mind plans were being made to throw over a million American soldiers and marines on to the beaches of Honshu to destroy those who would not admit defeat.

About this time some war weary souls high in the echelons of naval intelligence began to wonder if such continued mayhem could not be stopped by informing the Japanese people of the futility of the continuing destruction of their homeland and the killing of their people. As a result of this thought, it came to pass that some sort of propaganda campaign was to be initiated for the purpose of conveying this message to the Japanese people.

We received instructions to report the identity of any POW who we believed might be inclined for humanitarian reasons to participate in such a propaganda program. Questions were added to our interrogation reports which were designed to identify such persons. Though never told, we believed that some POWs were broadcasting such messages to Japan from a radio station on Guam. I participated in one phase of this program that involved me in a unique and dramatic event.

In early June all of the language personnel at the camp were ordered to muster at the stockade after evening chow. Freshly pressed khaki was the uniform required. When we arrived at the front gate of the camp after chow, we found four trucks with the cargo areas covered with canvass. Each truck was manned by smartly dressed, armed MPs. A number of prisoners were being checked out of the camp and placed in the trucks. We immediately recognized them as being a group of officers recently brought in from Okinawa and from Iwo Jima. There was one colonel, several majors and an assortment of captains and a few naval officers. Each interpreter was assigned to a truck and told to stay with the POWs in that truck for the remainder of the evening. After everyone was loaded the canvass was pulled tight across the rear opening and the convoy moved out.

After a trip of about forty-five minutes, we debarked into an area of large tents stretched over rectangular frames such as are used for offices. It was now dark and a few lights illuminated a well-manicured headquarters set up with tight security. We were at the headquarters of the 21st Bombardment Group. This was the headquarters of General LeMay.

As the POWs were being unloaded, we were taken into a small office. A navy captain told us that the prisoners were to be shown aerial photographs of Japan taken a few days before by American planes. We would accompany the Japanese officers and answer their questions and note their reactions. This was obviously an attempt to show these prisoners that their homeland was being devastated and that future resistance was madness. Most prisoners simply would not believe that American planes were bombing Tokyo and that the Imperial Fleet was impotent. They would not believe that Bull Halsey had almost sailed his flagship into Tokyo Bay. This evening was designed to prove a point.

We were all taken to a large tent. At this time we were joined by two naval officers who appeared to be fluent in Japanese. I could hear them banter with the prisoners. Their Japanese was surely learned on the streets of Tokyo or in a mission school. The idiom was beautiful. I tried to remember the inflections. The prisoners were told what they were to see. We passed from a small ante-room into a large area. The walls were covered with aerial photographs. Some were large composites and others were of small areas. Tables set in the center of the room were covered with photographs. These were aerial photographs taken a few days before by American planes flying over Japan. Picture after picture depicted the terrible damage being daily wreaked upon the Japanese cities by American super-fortresses.

For a moment the Japanese officers hung back, hesitant, afraid to look, not wanting to accept the inevitable truth. One officer walked to a table, leaned over and exclaimed, "Look! It's Yokohama" (Yokohama, Mita No?). The tension was broken. The prisoners spread out going from one set of photographs to another. The photos were arranged by locality – Tokyo, Nagasaki, Yokosuka, Sasebo, etc. The POWs, chastened, talked quietly among themselves. These Asian supermen were incredulous. Could it have come to this? Where were the mighty battleships, sleek cruisers and fast carriers that had left the American Pacific Fleet in flames at Pearl Harbor a little more than three years before? Where were the famous Zero fighters that had outperformed every American plane? These were not civilian soldiers, but military men well trained in aerial photograph interpretation. They knew the truth.

Soon, they were moving about pointing out places which they recognized.

"That's the officer's club at Yokohama." "Look, there is our barracks at Sasebo."

"Look at Tokyo. That's where my grandmother used to live."

"That's the airfield at Yokosuka. I flew out of there just about nine weeks ago."

For an hour or more, the Japanese officers poured over the exhibits asking questions and commenting on the quality of the work. Every one of them noticed that the grounds of the Imperial Palace in Tokyo had not been touched by American bombers.

"At what altitude were these taken?"

"Did the planes encounter anti-aircraft fire?"

"Did any fighters appear?"

One of the older photographs showed the super battleship Yamato, the largest battleship ever built. A naval officer who had once served aboard the leviathan pointed it out with pride. He was told that the ship was sunk off Okinawa a month before.

Soon it was time to depart. Without any ceremony, we boarded the trucks and headed back to the stockade. The Japanese were quiet. Hardly a word was said on the return trip. The POWs were delivered to the guards at the camp. Each one bowed goodnight – <u>O Yasumi nasai</u>. Surely there was little sleep to be had by any of them that night. The Greater East Asia Co – Prosperity Sphere lay in shreds all over the Pacific. They must be wondering whether or not the Empire itself would survive.

Banzai – One Thousand Years Had Ended.

In a few months the War was ended. The atomic bomb replaced the million men that McArthur and Nimitz were to hurl onto the beaches of the Japanese homeland. The awesome power of the bomb that burst over Hiroshima demonstrated to the Japanese people the futility of continued resistance. To have further reminded them of this would have been redundant. The propaganda campaign was shelved and consigned to the history books as an idea whose time had passed.

CHAPTER 7

"No matter what may happen,
whatever may befall,
I only know I'm mighty glad
I'm living, that is all."

I'M MIGHTY GLAD I'M LIVING
GEORGE M. COHAN

WE WERE APPROACHING THE FOURTH summer of the War. I had been in the Pacific theatre for fifteen months. The days were endless. We were bored, tired, frustrated, angry and homesick. There seemed to be no end to the war. Marines were usually not rotated back to the States until they had served twenty-four months overseas. I had a long way to go.

Everyone knew that the next major operation against the main islands of Japan was being planned. We were certain that it would include us. The Kamikaze attacks against the United States Fleet off Okinawa were enough to convince even the most optimistic observer that a lot of killing remained to be done. Any nation that could convince hundreds of young aviators to strap themselves into an airplane loaded with explosives and crash dive onto the deck of an enemy battleship would not go down easily. Every Marine that I knew firmly believed that we would be in the Pacific for years.

President Roosevelt died on April 13. I was in the prison infirmary when a POW came up to me and said, "America no daitoryo wa shinimashita." I knew that some American had died. I did not know that <u>daitoryo</u> was the word for President. He was first elected in 1933 when I was eight years old. Most of us had known no other President. The troops were sincerely sad. He had fought the good fight. We believed in his wisdom. After all, we were winning the war.

A Korean by the name of Kang Chu Bong, an inmate, was assigned to duty as a messenger and general handyman at the stockade office. The troops called him Butch Roosevelt. The day after FDR's funeral he became Butch Truman.

Seventeen days after the President's death, Adolf Hitler placed a cyanide pill between his teeth and shot himself in the head in a bunker beneath the Chancellery Building in Berlin. On May 8th Germany surrendered. The War in Europe was over. V-E Day had little effect on the troops in the Pacific. The War in Europe had never been our responsibility.

During the middle of June, a notice had appeared on the battalion bulletin board advising the troops that applications were being accepted for the Navy V-12 College Training Program. Under this program qualified applicants from the Navy and Marine Corps were sent to colleges and universities throughout the United States to be educated at government expense. Its purpose was to assure the Navy of a continuous supply of college educated men as officer candidates. The Navy was preparing for a long war. If selected, I would be transferred back to the States and assigned to a university of my choice for an education to be paid for by the Navy. A more accurate definition of paradise could hardly exist for a Marine Corporal who had survived fifteen months of war and whose future was sure to include an assault landing on the beaches of Honshu. I immediately filed an application for this program.

I had unsuccessfully applied for this program on Tinian one year earlier. In addition to this effort, I had also maintained some correspondence with Congressman Brooks about an appointment to West Point. A letter from his office that reached me after the campaign in the Marshalls had indicated that my request was still being considered. There were several well qualified applicants for V-12 in our battalion and the chance of being selected seemed rather slim.

The daily routine of the stockade continued. Some days I spoke more Japanese than English. The POWs started a kabuki theater and we helped them stage performances. I worked at developing my language skills. I even learned to tell a joke in Japanese. Humor is the ultimate of bilingual accomplishment. The prisoners began to learn English. Negro troops from an engineer unit often took the POWs out on work details. After a few days of such association, scatological comments in heavy southern dialect began to be heard interspersed with Japanese. Sum-bitch de gozaimas - - - Hey, mother san, baka!

On July 31 I was called to battalion headquarters and told that I had been selected for the V-12 Program and was scheduled to depart Guam by plane in two days. The news was given to me by a clerk who unemotionally handed me a copy of the order. I thought that ruffles and flourishes would have been in order. It was the most important message that I had ever received.

This was incredible news. I walked back to the stockade. I was going home. I sat on my bunk in our hut almost too happy to move. My God! I was going home. I had survived. At least for a while. I was going home to college – to safety – girls – books – to fresh vegetables – clean white sheets – to Mom and Dad – and apple pie and with luck, a ripe old age.

I was going home! Not by ship but by plane. I would be in the States in a week – home in two weeks. There was no time to write my Mother and Father. Their surprise would be my joy. My mates at the POW camp were happy at my good fortune. They all gave me messages to pass on to their wives and families when I arrived in the States. I had some doubts about going. Kraft and I had been together for a long time. It seemed strange that he should stay. I would miss him.

I packed my sea-bag, said farewell to my friends and on August 5 boarded a C-24 and flew out of Guam for home. We flew via Kwajalein and Johnston Islands making brief stops for fuel and arrived on Oahu during the first days of August.

On Tinian I had acquired a navy issue .45 caliber automatic pistol by trade with a navy ensign. I had carried it through the jungle patrols on Tinian and while serving at the POW camp on Guam. I carried it in a holster on my belt. No one had ever questioned my ownership. As I approached the processing center at the airfield on Oahu, an M.P. told me that it would be taken away from me as it was Navy issue. He suggested a trade. For my automatic he gave me a .38 caliber pistol which was not government issue. I was allowed to keep it. I still have it. It has not been fired since I acquired it.

After a week of processing and waiting, we were embarked on the U.S.S. President Monroe and set sail for San Francisco. This was the third time that I had departed Pearl Harbor by Navy transport. The two preceding trips were to hostile shores. This time the natives would be friendly. Fisherman's Wharf was secure.

A great many things happened between the time of my departure from Guam and my arrival in San Francisco. The atomic bombs were dropped on Hiroshima and Nagasaki and the Emperor had announced the Japanese surrender. The war was over. Our ship docked at Treasure Island the day after V-J Day.

While we were one day out from San Francisco, the Captain had announced the news of the Japanese surrender over the ship's speaker. The troops were elated in a quiet sort of way. My elation was muted. I had already experienced the thrill of going home. We were approaching the coast of California and soon the lights would be visible. After evening chow, most of us went on deck to watch for the lights of the Golden Gate bridge. I stayed up most of the night watching the lights on shore as they welcomed us home.

The seas were heavy as we approached the coast. The bow of the big transport seemed to rise hundreds of feet on each wave and then plunged deep into the dark sea beneath. I knew no one on the ship and had no one with whom to share my thoughts. I sat under a life boat and watched the lights glimmering from the shore. It was over. The war was finished. The great adventure was complete. We had been a part of it for so long that it now seemed that something was missing. We had been programmed for a long time.

Now the world was new. We needed new goals, new reasons and new stimuli. I knew that never again in my life would I become involved in so tremendous an undertaking. We had been a part of things the like of which we had never even dreamed.

Stephen Crane's young Civil War Soldier shared my thoughts:

"The youth was in a little trance of astonishment. So they   were at last going to fight. On the morrow perhaps there would be a battle and he would be in it. For a time, he was obliged to labor to make himself believe. <u>He could not accept with assurance an omen that he</u> <u>was about to mingle in one of these great affairs of the earth.</u>

He had of course dreamed of battles all of his life – of vague and bloody conflicts that had thrilled him with their sweep and fire. In visions, he had seen himself in many struggles. He had imagined peoples secure in the shadow of his eagle-eyed prowess. But awake he had regarded battles as crimson blotches on the pages of the past. He had put them as things of the bygone with his thought-images of heavy crowns and high castles. There was a portion of the world's history which he had regarded as the time of wars, but, it, he thought, had been long gone over the horizon and had disappeared forever." (Stephen Crane, <u>The Red Badge of Courage).</u>

Some of our youthful dreams had come true. It had happened. I had gone to war, I had fought battles. I had engaged in great movements that shook the world. I had participated in marches, sieges and conflicts. I had survived.

The memories would follow us all of our days. The experience would mold our thoughts, govern our emotions and haunt our dreams. We would talk about it and tell our tales as old soldiers have always done. Memories fade as young soldiers become old. Names and numbers and places and faces fade into the mists of the past. Only the history remains for others to read.

We spent a short time in San Francisco awaiting transport to the East Coast. I called my Mother and delighted in her surprise that I was safe at home in the States. Liberty in San Francisco after so many months in the Pacific was an exciting experience. We rediscovered the world of civilization. We accustomed ourselves to the fact that two genders still existed. The endless supply of girls was difficult to handle. For so many months girls in the form of nurses or an occasional entertainer were off-limits to enlisted men. As with most other enjoyable aspects of life, female companionship had been reserved for the Officers Club.

The need for future officers was ended and the Corps did not know what to do with the V-12 candidates. We were assigned to Camp Lejeune in North Carolina and in early September boarded a Southern Pacific train for transport to that base. On September 6th the train roared through Shreveport at sixty miles an hour. I could almost see my house, but homecoming was yet to be.

Upon arrival at Camp Lejeune the V-12 applicants were given an option of immediate discharge or assignment to the Officer Candidate School at Quantico, Virginia. After three months of training, we would be commissioned as Second Lieutenants and then discharged. The prospect of a commission as a Marine Officer was tempting, but I decided to accept the discharge.

I wanted to return to college as soon as possible. I was anxious to return to L.S.U. for the spring semester which would begin in February of 1946. Had I accepted the commission, I would have been a Reserve Officer and would have been recalled to active duty in five years to serve in Korea. This story could have ended in a different fashion.

On October 1, 1945, I stepped in front of a Marine Colonel, saluted and was handed a discharge from the United States Marine Corps, together with cash in the sum of $276.10 representing my accumulated pay and mustering out bonus.

We were transported to the front gate of Camp Lejeune and told to get off the bus. We were on our own. It was a strange new world that we re-entered. Sixty days before in the skies over Hiroshima a B-29 pregnant with uranium had given birth to the Atomic Age.

From Camp Lejeune, I took a bus to the Marine Base at Quantico, Virginia for a short visit with my brother Jim, who was a marine lieutenant teaching officer candidates how to fire mortars. He had been stationed at Quantico since his return from the South Pacific in 1943.

A few days later I hitched a ride with a newly discharged marine to St. Louis where I boarded the Southern Belle and headed home. I arrived in

Shreveport on October 7, 1945 to be greeted by my Mother and younger brother, Robert. We drove to my Father's Texaco station. He closed the business and we all went home. For us, the War was over.

Three days later, I was back on the Greenwood Road pumping gas and thinking about college.

> "Then darkness enveloped the whole American armada. Not a
> pinpoint of light showed from those hundreds of ships as they
> surged on through the night toward their destiny, carrying
> across the ageless and indifferent sea tens of thousands of young
> men, fighting for . . . for . . . well, at least for each other."

BRAVE MEN (1944)
ERNIE PYLE

NOTES
AND
BIBLIOGRAPHY

I have in my library a facsimile of <u>Fourteen Hundred and 91 Days in the Confederate Army</u> by W.W. Heartsill (Journal of the W.P. Lane Rangers from April 19, 1861 to May 20, 1865.) The original copy which had been given to my Grandfather by Heartsill in 1876 was in my father's possession for many years. I read it when I was in high school in Shreveport. My Grandfather's picture appears on page 127. Sometime after my father's death, the book was acquired by my cousin, Judge Claude Williams, who donated it to the Baylor University Library.

A fairly accurate description of the campaign in the Marshalls as well as the battles for Saipan and Tinian can be found in <u>To the Marianas</u> (1980 Van Nostrand Reinhold Co.), Edwin P. Hoyt. At page 80 of this volume is a description of the attack on the 3rd Battalion Command Post at Eniwetok which I wrote about in Chapter 3. Hoyt is wrong as to time. The attack occurred in the early morning shortly after dawn.

Samuel Eliot Morison's <u>History of United States Naval Operations in World War II, Vol. 7, Aleutians, Gilberts and Marshalls</u> contains an excellent commentary on the Banzai attack on the 3rd Battalion Command Post on the morning of February 20, 1944 on Eniwetok (pp. 298-299). Morison's account of the Catchpole Operation is excellent. In <u>Volume 8</u> of his history he covers the Marianas campaign in like fashion. In <u>Volume 7</u> there is a photograph of the third wave of assault boats about to hit the beach at Engebi. I was in one of these LCVPs.

I also used some information as to casualties and dates from Marine Corps Historical Reference Series No. 31, <u>The United States Marines in the Marshalls Campaign</u> (Revised 1962). I also made reference to <u>Tinian</u> and <u>The Seizure of Saipan</u>, by Gabrielle Neufeld, Historical Branch, G-3 Division Headquarters, United States Marine Corps, March 5, 1969.

AFTERWORD

This book was written by our father, Allen J. Tillery, who died in 2017 at age 92, as a memoir of his experiences as a soldier in the U.S. Marine Corps in World War Two including service in combat in the Pacific theater.

In 1943 Allen J. Tillery withdrew from college at L.S.U. and enlisted in the U.S. Marine Corps. The Corps sent him to language school and he served as a Japanese interpreter for the 22nd Marine Regiment in the Pacific war. He interrogated prisoners and participated in amphibious landings and combat in the Marshall and Mariana Islands and the pacification of Tinian and Guam.

This is the personal account of a young man from Shreveport, Louisiana who in 1943, like many young Americans looking forward to all of the good things in life available to them, put his dreams on hold and answered his country's call. When America was attacked by evil men with massive armies dedicated to the destruction of our freedoms it needed young men like him for an army to repel those who would destroy us. So he and millions of other young men signed on, picked up their rifles and went to war having little appreciation of the danger that they faced. They fought, bled and died by the thousands before victory was attained.

Today few of these young boys survive as their generation is passing into history. When you see the flags on their caskets remember what each one did to deserve it: put aside hopes and dreams, put on a uniform and went to war for all of us. These were no ordinary men. They deserve to be remembered as soldiers who answered their country's call. Their children and grandchildren must know, and we honor them by remembering, who they were and what they did so long ago.

A. Scott Tillery
M. Kelly Tillery
Jefferson R. Tillery

February 2018

stillery@bellsouth.net   – A. Scott Tillery
tilleryk@pepperlaw.com   – M. Kelly Tillery
jtillery@joneswalker.com   – Jeff R. Tillery

SEARCH PARTIES ON JANUARY 30 1945

SEARCH AREA	PARTIES NO.	PEOPLE SEARCHED FOR
Marupo point (508)	4	4
Above Marupo well (539,540)	2(women)	1
Kahi 7 han (Pepenogol 554, 555, 543, 544) (Sea-side of old Japanese air field area)	7	6

TOSHIO,YAMASHINA
Director,
Japanese Search Parties

Mr. Martin
Dear sir
How are you I heard you wounded. I am anxous
about your health.
I am moving cyclopédia of all inside Japan.
Please, report my name to your general of
information-bureau for inter-national piece
and humans happyness.
Yours faithfully.
S. Abe

1355/JLA-jap
Serial No. 734

HEADQUARTERS,
ISLAND COMMAND,
TINIAN, MARIANAS ISLANDS.

R E S T R I C T E D

5 February 1945

From: Island Commander,
To: Second Lieutenant Walter B. HARRISON (032371), U. S. Marine
           Corps Reserve.

Subject: Commendation.

1.   The outstanding work of the G-2 (Marine) Intelligence
Patrol, of which you were a leader, merits commendation from this headquarters.

2.   The resourceful and aggressive work of this patrol from
1 August 1944 to its disbandment on 1 February 1945 has often been over
and above that normally called for in the line of regular duty. This
patrol, a volunteer unit from the beginning, operating with a complement
of specialists such as photographers, aerial photo-interpreters, Japanese
interpreters, combat correspondent, general duty personnel and only two
classified scout-snipers, was always ready and available on short notice
to investigate or engage any reported enemy activity in areas throughout
the island not normally assigned to combat forces. The more than 140
missions of this unit have accounted directly for 33 known military dead,
7 prisoners of war captured, and the liberation of 96 or more civilians.
In addition, the intelligence information supplied to other units has
accounted for a great number of enemy military killed and civilians saved
for rehabilitation, as well as the destruction of enemy bivouac areas
and supplies. The patrol, which suffered some casualties while continu-
ally operating over strange terrain rife with enemy snipers and groups
of well armed enemy soldiers, also collected valuable information which
added much to the security of this island and its installations.

3.   The records of this headquarters indicate that the following named personnel of the G-2 Section were members of this patrol and
actively participated in a large number of combat missions.'

GySgt.	MARCUS, Saul	(392422)	Corp.	MELONI, Joseph E.	(926277)
Sgt.	BIGGS, Robert F. (Patrol Leader)	(303363)	Corp.	TILLERY, Allen J.	(841175)
			Corp.	TOMASSI, Louis P.	(564401)
Sgt.	DAVIS, Henry J., Jr. (Patrol Leader)	(376300)	PFC	DAVIS, Lonnie R.*	(520945)
			PFC	EVANS, Moce	(894948)
Sgt.	BENSON, Harold R.	(431617)	PFC	JENSEN, Milton S.	(498970)
Sgt.	CHAPEL, Norman	(373410)	PFC	LETCHER, Carl D.	(516427)
Sgt.	McKEAN, Richard L.	(348456)	PFC	LARKIN, William I.	(587855)
Corp.	GOODMAN, Travis L.	(504041)	PFC	OSGOOD, Fred N.	(470344)
Corp.	HAYMAN, Ted H.	(456808)	Pvt.	DUNCAN, Herbert V.	(864876)
Corp.	KRAFT, Robert A.	(864846)	Pvt.	LARSEN, Neil	(545831)

* Deceased

4.   It is with extreme pleasure that I commend you and the
above listed personnel for your outstanding and courageous work during
the above mentioned period.

- 1 -

ltr subject "Commendation" - Cont'd.

5.   A copy of this letter will be forwarded to the Commandant of the Marine Corps for file with your official record and a copy will be placed in the service record book of each of the men mentioned in paragraph 3 above.

/s/ Frederick V. H. Kimble,
FREDERICK V. H. KIMBLE,
Brig. Gen., U. S. Army.

Copy to: CMC; SRB each man concerned.

CERTIFIED A TRUE COPY:

A. L. PERRY,
CWO, USA
Asst Adj Gen

- 2 -

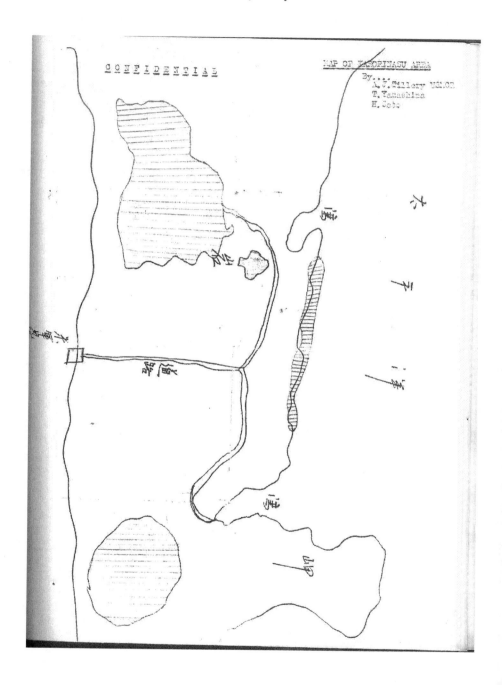

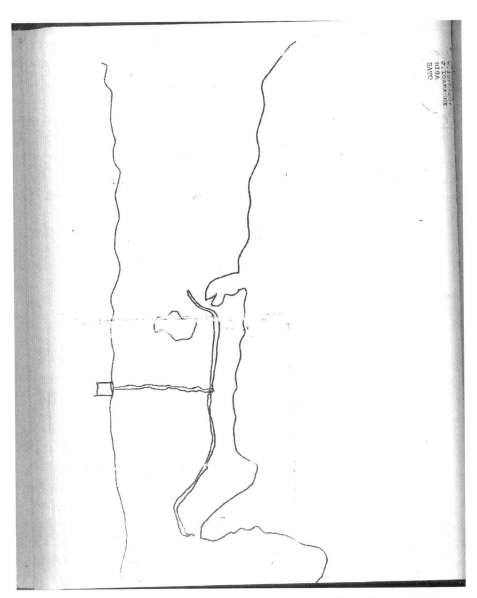

Map of Karorinasu Area, near Marupo Springs Tinian where Corporal Allen J. Tillery and 15 man patrol encountered several Japanese soldiers in a cave, August 15, 1944 – drawn by Corporal Allen J. Tillery, U.S.M.C., Toshio Yamashina, Deputy Mayor and Hataya Sato, Mayor of Camp Churo, Tinian

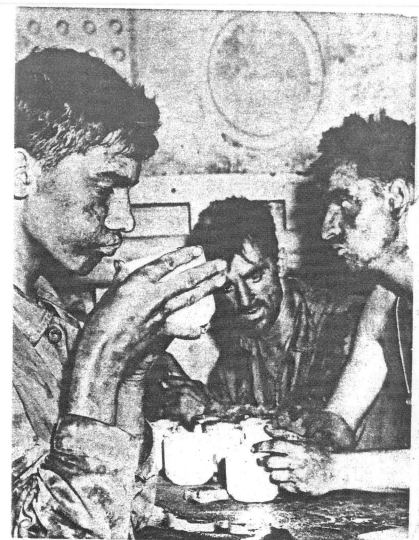

ALMIGHTY GOD:
Our sons, pride of our nation,

More Japs Killed On Island After Battle Than During It

By HARRY STROUP

SOMEWHERE IN THE MARIANAS, Feb. 18—(Delayed)—When Maj. Charles Erb Jr., one-time "won-lan" grid team" star and command, invited me to Island company a patrol on a "Jap hunt," I anticipated a little excitement.

Japs had been reported as having been seen in a cave down the coast, and we cruised along close to shore in a picket boat looking for them, but had no luck. Later we went out again on another two-hour cruise looking for a stolen fishing boat but still no luck, not even at fishing.

I hit the sack at midnight after attending a little shindig, given by Maj. "Dixie" Thompson of the Air Corps in honor of the arrival of his baby daughter, and was just about to fall asleep when there came the report of machine gun fire not far from my tent. I rolled over once or twice and awoke this morning to learn—you guessed it—a couple of Japs had been shot not far from where I lay snoozing. One was killed and the other, an air corps warrant officer in the Jap navy, was wounded twice and is now in the hospital.

Thousands Killed

Night firing is commonplace here and it usually means that one or more Japs have joined their ancestors. There is nothing much you can do except to stay in your tent, as it isn't "healthy" to go prowling about in the dark here when there is shooting going on.

As a matter of fact, more Japs have been killed since this island was declared secure on August 1, 1944, than were killed in the battle for the island. Approximately 4,000 were killed in the fight for the island and another 7,000 since then, according to the reports.

Picked patrols are continuing the work of cleaning out the Japs, and it is estimated that a hundred or more soldiers are still hiding out in the many caves which dot the island. They come out at night in search of food or clothing and have been known to raid mess supplies

is now a first lieutenant in the Air Corps. Another brother, Capt. Henry Weinstraub was taken prisoner by the Germans in North Africa and has recently been exchanged. The Weinstraub boys make their home in Brooklyn, N. Y. They are also well known in Minneapolis, Minn.

Well Known Author

The patrol was formerly under command of Col. Clyde H. Metcalf of the Marines. He was succeeded by Major Erb. Colonel Metcalf is a well known author and a veteran of 30 years in the Marine Corps. At present he is stationed at Pearl Harbor. It was Colonel Metcalf's practice to accompany the patrols on all missions, and Major Erb is continuing this policy.

The patrol has made a total of 140 missions, killing 100 Japs and taking ten prisoners of war. In addition to this work the interpreters attached to the patrol have been instrumental in convincing a large number of civilian Japs to surrender, the record shows.

Of the original patrol of 14 men only six are still on the island. They are:

Marine Sgt. H. J. Eavis of Philadelphia veteran of the Guadalcanal fighting.

Sgt. R. F. Biggs of Fenton, Mich.

Sgt. Herman Chapel of Norfolk, Va., Marine Combat correspondent attached to intelligence. Sergeant Chapel saw action a t Guadalcanal and on other Pacific Islands and has won a reputation for his fine descriptive stories, some of them written under fire. He was a member of the editorial staff of the Norfolk Ledger-Dispatch for six years prior to joining the Marine Corps.

Marine Cpl. J. E. Meloni of Wellesley, Mass.

Marine Cpl. R. A. Kraft of Seattle, Wash., interpreter.

Marine Cpl. A. J. Tillery of Shreveport, La., interpreter.

Dangerous Work

Kraft is 19 years old and Tillery just 20, but both are accomplished linguists and veteran fighters. Their work is usually dangerous, as they must head the patrols in

Jap hunting is dangerous work, and experienced men only are permitted to engage in this task. The mixed Army-Marine patrol attached to the Island Command of Brig. Gen. Frederick V. H. Kimble has been recommended for a citation in connection with their part in this important campaign. Members of this patrol, now commanded by Maj. Gen. Erb, have all seen action in various Pacific island campaigns, including the taking of Tinian, Tarawa, Guadalcanal and the Marshalls.

Leader Killed

The original patrol leader, Lt. Dale Chamberlin of the Marines, was killed three months ago while on night ambush duty. Killed in the same action was Marine Pfc. L. K. Davis. Lt. Chamberlin was killed by a Jap grenade, while Davis died of wounds from an automatic weapon.

Two other marines attached to the patrol have been wounded and sent home for recuperation. They are Gunnery Sgt. Saul Marcus and Pfc. W. I. Martin, interpreter. Marcus suffered shrapnel wounds in the chest, a missile piercing one lung. Martin received severe body wounds when the Japs opened up from a cave on which the patrol was advancing. He was in the lead and had been calling to the enemy troops in Japanese, urging them to surrender.

After Chamberlin's death Lt. W. B. Harrison, of Seattle, Wash., became patrol leader, serving in this capacity for several months and accounting for a long string of Japs. He played center on the University of Washington football team in 1941-42 and '43 and was also on the crew there. Lt. Harrison's wife and baby daughter reside in Seattle.

Maj. Sam Weinstraub of the 2nd Command is another Army representative on the patrol. His father, Milt Weinstraub, played professional baseball with the Sioux Falls team in the Western league and for other minor league teams in the East. He was with the Boston Senators for several weeks before giving up a promising big league career to join the Army. He

the assaults on the Jap hideouts. Very often their efforts to induce the Japs to surrender are answered by rifle fire or a barrage of hand grenades.

The intelligence work done by these two fine youngsters has been of great help to the authorities in determining the policy to be followed in dealing with the Japs, both military and civilian.

Major Erb is high in his praise of the work done by the entire group. Charley served in the Marines during the first World War and is probably one of the few Army officers who knows how to work with Marines. The boys are all fully conversant with Charley's fine record as an athlete and look upon him as their coach as well as leader.

As every sports fan knows, Charley called the signals for the University of California "wonder team" from 1922 to 1924, leading an outfit that never knew defeat in three years of playing. As a coach he has made a reputation that puts him in the class of other football "greats." Today, although he is busy fighting a war and has seen service in more than one Pacific Theater, Charley still talks football and sports whenever he gets a chance.

Charley believes in the benefit of athletics from the standpoint of good health as well as for fun and recreation and he keeps to a regular training schedule.

What They Learn

Here are some of the things members of the patrol have learned about the Japs:

Many of the Jap soldiers commit suicide because if they are taken alive they are "considered dead" back in Japan and may never return. This was brought out when certain Jap prisoners begged that their capture not be reported to Japan. Civilian Japs on the other hand have taken their lives by jumping over "suicide cliff," or by other means, because they believed they would be tortured and killed by the Americans.

The Jap soldier is tough and wiry, but he is no match for the average American fighter.

The fanatical belief in Hirohito by the Jap fighting man and in ultimate victory for Japan, is being shattered by the success of the American forces in the Pacific.

<u>USEFUL JAPANESE WORDS AND PHRASES</u>
(Compiled by G-2 Section, to be used by "chasers" in charge of Japanese
        working parties)

<u>PRONOUNCIATION</u>

        The vowels are pronounced as in Spanish, Italian, German, etc.
a is pronounced ah as in farm.
e   "   eh   "   bed.
i   "   ee   "   police.
o   "   oh   "   boa6
u   "   oo   "   rude

        The consonants are pronounced as in English.
        Accent the capitalized syllables. Pronounce the others in a mono-
tone.

Advance	SU-su-me
At ease	YA-su-me
Come here	ko-chi ko-i
Come out	de-te ko-i
Come with me	o-i-de
Enter, get in	ha-I-te
Give me	a-GE-te
Halt	to-MA-re
Hurry	ha-YA-ku
Immediately	su-gu ni
Later	a-to de
Quiet	da-MA-re
Wait	cho-to
Yes (yes)	HA-i
(that's right)	SO des
(I have. There are.)	v-ri-mas
No (no)	i-YE
(that's wrong)	chi-GA-i-mas
(there aren't any)	a-ri-ma-son
"	NA-i des
Please	do-zo
"	CHO-dai
Thanks	a-ri-ga-to
What?	NAN da
Where?	do-ko
Airplane	hi-KO_ki
Cigarette	ta-ba-ko
Hole, cave	a-na
Money	KA-ne (YEN #.... SEN ¢)
Shovel, tool	DO-gu
Water	MI-zu
Have you eaten?	ta-be-ta ka
Do you speak English?	E-i-go ga de-ki-mas ka
How old are you?	TO-shi wa... ik'sa-i des ka
Head	BEN-jo
Where's the head?	BEN-jo wa....do-ko des ka
I have to go to the head.	SHO-ben shi-ta-i
American.	a-me-ri-ka-jin
Jap	ni-hon-jin
Korean	CHO-sen-jin
Okinawan	o-ki-na-wa
U.S.M.C.	(a-me-ri-ka no) ri-ku sen-tai
Soldier	HE-i-ta-i
Civilian	min-kan

Numbers				
1	i-chi	10		ju
2	ni	11		ju i-chi
3	san	12		ju ni
4	shi	13		ju san
5	go	20		ni ju
6	ro-ku	30		san-ju
7	na-na	40		shi ju
8	ha-chi	100		hya-ku
9	ku	1000		is-sen

/1990-85(2)
6127/274

745

R E S T R I C T E D

HEADQUARTERS,
FIFTH AMPHIBIOUS CORPS,
c/o FLEET POST OFFICE, SAN FRANCISCO

13 January, 1944.

From: The Commanding General.
To :   Corporal Allen J. TILLERY, (641175), USMC-SS.

Subject: Orders.

Reference: (a) SecNav Restricted Ltr 1990-85 over DFA-321-pbf,
             dated 31Aug43.

1.   You will, on this date, report to the Commanding
Officer of a previously designated ship for transportation to
such place where the 22d Marines (Reinforced) may be, reporting
upon arrival to the Commanding Officer, that Regiment, for duty.

2.   Your staff returns will be forwarded by mail.

3.   There being no travel involved in the execution
of these orders, other than government transportation provided,
none is authorized.

S. A. Guy
S. A. GUY,
By direction.

Copy to: CMC;   PM;   CO,CorpsHqTrs (5);   CO,22dMar(Reinf)
           (5); Corps Postal O;   G-2;   Corp TILLERY (10);
           F I L E.

R E S T R I C T E D

Hq, 22d Marines (Rein), 5th A C   1st Endorsement   13 January 1944

From: The Commanding Officer.
To: Corporal Allen J. Tillery (241175), USMC-SS.

Subject: Orders.

1.   Reported this date. You will further report to the
Commanding Officer, Headquarters and Service Company, for duty.

C. C. CALLAN,
By direction.

HEADQUATERS COMPANY,
FIRST BASE HEADQUARTERS BATTALION,
FLEET MARINE FORCE, PACIFIC
C/O FLEET POST OFFICE
SAN FRANCISCO, CALIFORNIA

10 July 1945

From: Corporal Allen J. TILLERY, 841175, USMCR
TO: The Commanding Officer, Headquarters Company, First Base Headquarters
Battalion, Fleet Marine Force, Pacific.

Subject: Consideration for assignment to College Training Program, request for.

Reference: (a) Letter of Instruction No. 1035
(b) Letter of Instruction No. 878
(c) Fleet Marine Force Special Order No. 166-45

1.   It is requested that I be considered for assignment to the college
Training Program.

2.   I have completed the following school work:
Graduated from Fair Park High School, Shreveport, Louisiana on 1 May 1942 with creditable scholarship rating. I have successfully completed four (4) years of high school
mathematics in the fields of algebra, geometry, trigonometry, and commercial arithmetic
Completed first semester, first year college at Louisiana State University on 1
February 1943, where I was a cndidate for the degree of Bachelor of Science, and
majoring in Electrical Engineering. This is the extent of my formal education.

3.   I was born at Shreveport Louisiana on 31 January 1925. I am a citizen
of the United States by reason of birth.

4.   I am unmarried, and agree to remain unmarried until commissioned
unless released by the Navy Department.

5.   If I am selected for this training I agree to change in rank to prive

6.   A copy of my Birth Certificate under seal of office of issue, and
a certified transcript of my high school record are on record with my official
record at Headquarters Marine Corps.

ALLEN J. TILLERY

3..
                    UNITED STATES MARINE CORPS
                         HEADQUARTERS
                 SOUTHERN PROCUREMENT DIVISION
                    PUBLIC RELATIONS SECTION
                      50 Whitehall Street
                      Atlanta, 3, Georgia

     The enclosed news story is sent to you with the
compliments of the United States Marine Corps.

     A copy of this story has been sent to all your
local newspapers. If you should obtain an extra copy of
the papers in which it is published, we would appreciate
it if you would send it to us for our clipping files,
giving us the name and date of the paper.

                         Sincerely,

                         RUTH D. BAUMGARTNER
                         1st Lieutenant, MCWR

N E W S
OF THE
UNITED STATES MARINES

FROM PUBLIC RELATIONS SECTION.
U. S. MARINE CORPS.
SOUTHERN PROCUREMEMT DIVISION.
1101-13 ATLANTA NATIONAL BUILDING
50 WHITEHALL STREET
ATLANTA 3. GA.

TINIAN, MARIANAS ISLANDS, October 00 (Delayed). --
Marine Corporal A. J. Tillery, of 2601 Quinton Street, Shreveport, La., participated in one of the patrols of the caves
of this island in search of elusive Japs.

Along with other members of Marine patrols assigned
to the task of cleaning out the Nipponese, he can testify
that it is a ticklish job.

On one patrol, the Marines were led to well-camouflaged
caves by two enemy internees. Corporal Tillery, arriving at
the cave, called out for the Japs to su render. They refused.
Then, in attempting to improve his cover, one of the Japs
stuck out his foot. It immediately was shot off by the arines.
Hand grenades finished the job, killing three enemy soldiers.
Two others were found in a nearby cave. They were suicides.

Three other Japs, outwardly dead, were lying on a low-
hanging ledge. The Marines learned on Guadalcanal that Japs
like to play dead. They sent a volley of fire into the supine
bodies. The three Japs leapt up only to slump to earth for
good as explosives cut them down.

Grenades were poured into another dugout. Four more
Japs were killed.

-USMC-

THE ARISAKA - FROM TOYO KOGYO TO PHILADELPHIA

By M. Kelly Tillery

As a young boy growing up in a quiet suburb of New Orleans, I often ventured into a dusty closet in the utility room adjacent to our carport. There, amongst numerous rakes, hoes, brooms, and miscellaneous tools was an out of place item – an implement of war from another time and place. A 7.7 mm, bolt action Japanese Army Type 99 Arisaka rifle.

It is an ominous weapon, yet not the quality of similar U.S. ordinance of its era. In that pre-Sony/Lexus time, "Made in Japan" had a decidedly different meaning than it does today. I often held this rifle for hours on end in my back yard and thought about the men who made it, the man to whom it was issued and who last fired it, and my father, U.S. Marine Corps Corporal Allen Jere Tillery (USMC No. 841175), one of the last men to be at the killing end of it. It inspired me to a life of inquiry about history, war, law, politics and why men act as they do.

Like many Baby Boomers, I often went to bed asking my father, "What did you do in the war, Daddy?" Yes, in the 1950's and even early 1960's "the" War was World War II. Korea was a "police action" and we still had the good sense to have only "advisors" in Vietnam. My father had lots of war stories to tell, as he served in the South Pacific Theatre for 2 ½ years fighting the Japanese Imperial Army at the point.

My brother and I listened wide-eyed to his tales of combat which always ended with him singing a lovely Japanese lullaby as we drifted off. While we dreamed of military adventures, my father prayed that his sons would never have to see what he had at 19 in the stinking jungles and bloody beaches of a half dozen Pacific islands. He always said he fought so we would not have to.

This weapon, the Arisaka, which came to inspire me has quite a history. It is named for Colonel Nariakira Arisaka (1852-1915), head of the Japanese commission which directed the development of a new army rifle in the 1890's. It was a considerable advancement over the rifle it replaced, the 8 mm Murata, the first indigenously produced Japanese rifle, in use since 1880. The Empire of Japan, less than 50 years earlier a closed, feudal society, was in the 1890's a rising industrial and military power which would soon, in 1905, shock the world by defeating the once mighty Russian Navy in the Russo-Japanese War. The Land of the Rising Sun had come a long way since 1853 when U.S. Admiral Matthew Perry sailed his "black ships" into Tokyo Bay and compelled that insular nation to open up, or be leveled by cannon fire. It did and Perry's insult was repaid with a vengeance on December 7, 1941.

From 1898 on, Japan produced over 6.4 million of various types of Arisakas before the last few shoddy, "last ditch" versions were cobbled together in July of 1945 from scrap as the Empire collapsed. It was state of the art for a long time, comparable to the British Lee-Enfield, the German Mauser or the American Springfield. It was the primary personal weapon of virtually every Japanese soldier on every God-forsaken island and atoll from Saipan and Tinian to Guam and Iwo Jima. U.S. Marines bearing superior, semi-automatic M-1 Garand rifles or carbines faced off against the Emperor's best bearing Arisakas.

The Arisaka is curious in several respects. Mine bears many scars of battle and has been fired many times, no doubt even killed one or more U.S. troops. The Type 99 includes a flip-down, wire monopod under the barrel to allow the user to steady the weapon to fire in the prone position. Unfortunately, the wire is rather flimsy and provides a wobbly firing platform. Many were removed and discarded as a nuisance in the field. It also has a unique safety, operated by pressing in the large knurled disc at the rear of the bolt and rotating it in a 1/8 clockwise turn. It also includes a rather optimistic, winged, "anti-aircraft" sight which theoretically permits the user to lead a speeding aircraft and shoot it down. Neither Corporal Tillery nor I are aware of any instance of a U.S. aircraft being shot by, much less downed by, an Arisaka. But it could take down a Marine at 400 meters.

The model I have, a Type 99, is so designated by the last two digits of the Japanese year of the reign of the then Emperor, Hirohito. Thus, in Japanese calendar year 2599, or Gregorian calendar year 1939, the Type 99 was first produced.

Though a spoil of war taken from an unwilling donor on the field of battle by a victor, and I having possession, it is, I suppose, technically still the property of the Emperor, now Akihito (son of Hirohito). Each Arisaka was originally stamped on its receiver with the symbol of The Emperor – a 16-petal Chrysanthemum, indicating that it was the property of the Emperor, not the soldier who carried it and not the Imperial Army.

However, only Arisakas, like mine, taken in the field still bear this gentle, but bold symbol. After the war, in one of its final standing orders, the Imperial Army Staff ordered that the Chrysanthemum be ground off all weapons before they were officially surrendered to U.S. forces, as a way of saving face. Short of a personal appeal accompanied by an apology, the Emperor will not be getting my Arisaka back anytime soon.

Mine bears the Chrysanthemum and the Kanji characters Shiki (Type) and Kojuko (99) on the top of the receiver.

It also bears a Serial Number with Armory designations: 87975

The first small symbol (kana) and number means this rifle was number 87,975 in Series 30, the first series of 100,000 manufactured in 1939, two years before Pearl Harbor and five years before August 15, 1944 when Corporal Tillery acquired it. The second symbol means it was produced at the Togo Kogyo Arsenal. It probably saw lots of action before its bearer met his demise on Tinian in 1944.

This arsenal was operated by a private contractor, Togo Kogyo Co., Ltd., a prominent manufacturer of machine tools and vehicles. It produced 557,000 Type 99 Arisakas between 1939 and 1945. In 1984, the company changed its name to Mazda Motor Corporation, now headquartered in Hiroshima. If I had known the same company that made this rifle also made my 1989 RX-7 sportscar, I would have bought a Ford.

It also includes an early model Type 30 Bayonet with a hooked quillion and markings indicating it was manufactured at another arsenal, the Kokura Arsenal in Kokura, Japan.

The 16 inch blade includes a "blood gutter". G.I. lore has it that this indentation along the length of the blade allows blood to seep out of a wound preventing a vacuum and permitting the attacker to easily withdraw it from a victim. In reality, it is merely a design feature to enhance strength of the blade. My father says he was taught in boot camp that the quickest way to remove your bayonet from a victim was to pull the trigger. Such was war at the point in 1944.

The ancient Japanese city of Kokura had been the primary target of the second atomic bomb drop ("Fat Man") on August 9, 1945. Major Charles Sweeney turned his B-29, "Bock's Car", towards Nagasaki, his secondary target, when he could not see Kokura, then obscured by clouds and smoke from the recent fire-bombing of nearby Yahata. Kokura had first been spared atomic infamy only three days before when Colonel Paul Tibbitts flying the "Enola Gay" found clear skies above Hiroshima to drop the first atomic bomb ("Little Boy") and needed not visit his secondary target, Kokura. My aunt Xenia Tillery, also a lawyer, tells me her uncle, Sgt. Joseph S. Stiborik was Tibbits' radar operator on that historic mission.

The Enola Gay took off that fateful day, August 6, 1945, at 2:45 AM, from North Field, Tinian Island about a year after the U.S. Marines obliterated a crack Japanese Army defending it. Shortly after the assault troops departed, Corporal Allen J. Tillery, serving as an interpreter with the 8th Marine Regiment Battalion Intelligence Section would encounter the bearer of my Arisaka on the opposite end of the island.

My father had been trained by the Marine Corps to kill Japanese soldiers, but also to speak and read Japanese in order to acquire intelligence from captured troops and often to persuade holdouts in the field to surrender. Today at 86, he still delights in surprising Japanese tourists with his rusty idiom. His vocabulary, however, is decidedly military, so he has to be reminded not to ask waiters at sushi restaurants how many Nambu machine guns are in the kitchen.

Tinian, in The Marianas, an island 12 miles long and 4 miles across was in 1944 defended by 9,000 battle-hardened Japanese Imperial Troops under command of Colonel Kioshi Ogata, a veteran of the Sino-Japanese War. His core 4,000 man 50th Regiment had seen lots of action in Manchuria. Although most perished at hands of U.S. Marine invaders, as many as 800 remained armed and hiding in caves throughout the island, ready to fight to the death for the Emperor. Surrender was disgrace. It was not an option.

It was just such a small group of Japanese soldiers that Corporal Tillery encountered that hot August 1944 day in a cave on the southern end of Tinian Island, in the face of a cliff on the Karorinasu plateau near Marupo Springs, the scene of fierce fighting not a few weeks before.

Tillery's 15 man patrol had been tasked with killing or capturing the soldiers hiding in the caves who had been firing on truck convoys at the base of the cliffs and whom had recently killed a Navy Sea-Bee driving a truck on the road. Perhaps this was the last kill of my Arisaka. In six months, the patrol would have over 140 encounters with Japanese troops like this first one.

The last shots from my Ariska fired in anger were directed to the point Marine at the head of this patrol on August 15, 1944. Two Japanese soldiers fired, missed and then retreated into the cave.

Corporal Tillery was given the unenviable job of crawling up the cliff to get near the cave to coax its denizens out. In his flawless and distinct Japanese, the Marine Corporal explained that the battle was over, they were surrounded, that if they put down their weapons and exited the cave with hands up, no harm would come to them and that to die now was useless. No sooner had the last foreign word passed the Marine's lips, did the soldiers yell "Banzai!", "Banzai!" and several hand grenades exploded in the cave. One tried to run out with weapon in hand, but was met with a hail of M-1 and Browning Automatic Rifle (BAR) fire.

When the smoke cleared, the distorted bodies of 4 or 5 Japanese soldiers were found near the mouth of the cave. They had committed Seppuku ("stomach-cutting" - the act of the dishonored samurai warrior disemboweling himself with a short sword – a tantō), though with the modern and more effective means of a hand grenade held against the belly.

The cave was filled with supplies, weapons and ammunition. They could have held out and killed more U.S. troops for a long time. In 1965, twenty years after the war ended, two Japanese soldiers wandered out of the jungle on Guam and surrendered to a local policeman.

All of the cave's contents were destroyed except a couple of Arisakas and a Nambu light machine gun which Corporal Tillery took with him. He gave one Arisaka to his tent mate who was an aide to a morale officer, and as such, had connections. The tent mate got a carpenter to build a crate to ship the two souvenirs to his mother in Nashville, Tennessee. She, in turn, shipped the Corporal's Arisaka to his mother (my grandmother) Lake Erie Johnston Tillery, in Shreveport, Louisiana, where the Corporal found it when he returned from war on October 7, 1945, nine years to the day before I was born.

The Corporal or Allen J. as I like to call him, married, moved to suburban New Orleans, and literally hung out his shingle to practice law above a bank on the Mississippi River, near smelly stockyards and an illegal casino. The Arisaka lay in storage, only to be found by my curious little hands at about the age of 10 which began my musings.

Hurricane Betsy hit New Orleans with a vengeance in 1965 and our home was flooded with 6 feet of muck, mire and Gulf water. Like my baseball card collection, my mother's silverware and almost all our household goods, the Arisaka was submerged in this toxic soup for a few days. We survived and rebuilt and I found the Arisaka. It was rusted, inoperable and generally a mess. I was saddened and knew my father would be, too.

I resolved to restore it and present to the Corporal. Though only 11 years old, I was rather handy, a fact which never ceases to amuse my children. I try to explain that facility with mechanical things does not necessarily translate to i-phones and computers.

I worked diligently in secret for several months on my project. When complete, the Arisaka looked almost new, except for the battle scars and was operable. I even bought some ammunition for it, but never did fire it. August 15, 1944, Marupo Springs, Tinian remains the last time and place this killing tool was fired.

When I presented it to the Corporal, I thought I saw a tear in the eye of the old Marine. He proudly kept it visible, near his books, in his library and I often sat holding it there and thinking.

Unbeknownst to me, not a few months before in June 1965, he had completed a manuscript about his war experiences, <u>Well and Smartly Done – A Remembrance of War, 1943-1945</u>. For reasons still unknown to me, he did not show it to me until 20 years later when he inscribed a bound copy, "For Kelly – a codification of all the war stories and sea-tales that you will never have to listen to again." It includes a vivid and detailed description of that fateful day when he acquired the Arisaka.

Fast forward 40 years to late August 2005 – Hurricane Katrina delivers a body blow to the New Orleans area, depositing up to 18 feet of water in my parents' home in Chalmette. Once again, the Arisaka joined their worldly goods under the deluge, this time for weeks.

Allen J. eventually retrieved the Arisaka from its damp and muddy resting place, but reported that it was an ugly, rusty mess. I asked him to ship it to me so I could try to restore it, again, as I had 40 years before. He did and I tried. But it was too far gone. Or at least beyond my humble ability to revive it.

I located a retired Marine, Ronald H. Morgan, near our vacation home in Vermont who restores weapons as a hobby. I brought him the patient and he promised to make it shine. And he did. The Corporal would be pleased.

I shall return to New Orleans soon and present the Arisaka to my father – again. Until then, I still often hold it and think of how grateful I am that some 56 year old Tokyo lawyer, son of a 50th Regiment Japanese soldier, is not sitting in his library holding my father's M-1.

M. Kelly Tillery
August 8, 2011

This article first appeared in THE PHILADELPHIA LAWYER, Vol. 77, No. 1, Spring 2014.

Made in the USA
Columbia, SC
12 December 2023

27589938R00088